THE REPAIR & RESTORATION OF POTTERY & PORCELAIN

THE REPAIR & RESTORATION OF POTTERY & PORCELAIN

Joan Grayson

 Sterling Publishing Co., Inc.   New York

Published in 1982 by
Sterling Publishing Co., Inc.
Two Park Avenue
New York, N.Y. 10016

ISBN 0-8069-5466-3

Published by arrangement with Evans Brothers, Ltd.
This edition available in the United States, and the
Philippine Islands only

Printed and bound in Great Britain
at The Pitman Press, Bath

CONTENTS

ACKNOWLEDGEMENTS

My thanks are due to my family who suggested I write this book during a prolonged period of enforced idleness as a result of an accident. I am grateful for the help and encouragement I received from them, and from so many of my students who thought it a good idea.

I would also like to express my gratitude to Mrs A. M. Wissler of Robin Hood's Workshop who originally set me on the path of teaching this subject.

Joan Grayson

At the beginning of each chapter is a list of tools, materials and equipment necessary for the particular stage of the work being described.

At the end of the book is a complete list of all tools, materials and equipment with the names and the addresses of suppliers.

U.S. equivalent names of materials and equipment are given in italics at the beginning of each chapter in the list of tools and equipment necessary, and also at their first mention in the chapter. A list of U.S. suppliers is included at the end of the book.

INTRODUCTION

Until recent times it was not possible to make a good repair on broken pieces of china in the home. Of this we constantly find evidence in salerooms, junk shops, and, of course, in our own homes. The old repair on that precious plate or heirloom, with its ugly line of ageing brown glue or a mass of unsightly rivets, is a poignant reminder of bygone efforts to preserve a much loved and valued piece. Today, however, thanks to the introduction of modern adhesives and other materials at relatively low cost, good home repairs are a very real possibility.

The restoration of broken china has been carried on for many centuries. The Chinese perfected a method of cutting down the broken necks of vases and binding the rims with metal. They also used the technique of painting in to conceal cracks and chips, and their repairs are very difficult to detect.

In Roman times, melted-down wax was used to camouflage cracks and chips and conceal damaged areas. The porcelain vendors of those days could be heard assuring their customers in the market place that their wares were *sine cera* (without wax), therefore undamaged, whole and genuine. It is interesting to reflect that our word 'sincere' possibly originates from the porcelain vendors of those times. At this point I do not think it amiss to impress upon anyone restoring china that you should aim to be sincere in your approach to the subject, for while experiencing the joy and satisfaction of seeing those many pieces of old and broken china building up under your hands to become whole and beautiful once more, you should not work in such a way as to deceive, presenting the restored piece as undamaged, whole and perfect. A restored ceramic should always be presented as a restored piece, put back together as perfectly as possible, but not deviating from the original piece for the sake of camouflage and concealment. You should approach this work with the intention that you are not only restoring and repairing, but you are also conserving.

Restoring china can become a most exciting and rewarding pastime. Searching in jumble sales, junk shops and auction rooms for damaged pieces to bring home and repair is in itself absorbing and fascinating. It is not unknown for a rare and valuable but damaged piece to be picked up at a low cost and, when repaired, to be not only a delight to behold, but also greatly increased in value.

For the collector of antique china this means that some pieces which would otherwise be out of his price range can now be added to his collection. For others, a hobby can become a profitable source of income, by repairing china for dealers, private collectors, or simply working for yourself, repairing and selling.

It is not necessary for the repairer to have had any artistic training, but a good sense of colour is important and a knowledge of sculpture can also be helpful. Perhaps the most important quality necessary in the repairer of porcelain is patience and plenty of it. This work requires a good deal of time. Do not think you can rush in from shopping, mix up some adhesive and put a few broken pieces together in between other jobs. It will require your full and undivided attention for many hours.

A restorer will need to know something about ceramics, so read as many books as you can on the subject, attend lectures on porcelain and pottery and go to exhibitions whenever possible. It is also necessary to acquire some books giving you potters' marks and monograms. As you handle the china you will gradually come to recognise the different wares.

It is of use to the restorer to know the basic difference between pottery and porcelain and the two different types of porcelain.

Porcelain

There are two distinct types of porcelain, hard paste and soft paste.

Hard paste The Chinese had the secret of making hard paste porcelain for many centuries and almost all Chinese porcelain falls into this category. Hard paste consists of china clay or kaolin and petuntse and is fired at a high temperature, $1,450°C$. This type of porcelain can be termed true porcelain.

European potters were not able to achieve the hard paste of Chinese porcelain until the early eighteenth century, when the Meissen factory near Dresden produced a good hard paste porcelain. Most German factories have been producing such porcelain since.

Soft paste Soft paste porcelain is made from white clay and ground glass frit and is fired at a much lower temperature than that required for hard paste porcelain. An important point to remember when using abrasive papers and files on repaired china, is that it is very easy to damage the surface of soft paste porcelain. Most continental porcelain is soft paste, as is that originating in the

British Isles, with the exception of Bristol, Plymouth and New Hall porcelain.

When dealing with broken pieces, you should note that the broken edges of soft paste have a granular texture, while those of hard paste have a hard glass-like texture.

Pottery

Pottery is an opaque earthenware, much softer and more porous than porcelain. Very early pottery pieces were often moulded by hand and fired at a very low temperature, or, in many cases, simply left to bake in the sun. Stoneware, slipware, Wedgwood, Staffordshire, and saltglaze (which, as the name implies, involved the introduction of salt into the kiln during firing) all come under the heading of pottery.

1. YOUR WORKROOM AND YOU

The ideal workroom should be a well lit, well ventilated room. It should have a large north-facing window with an extractor fan. The room should be large enough to take a good-sized workbench or table, plenty of shelves and a large cupboard, preferably steel, for the storage of toxic and inflammable materials and chemicals. A basin which is supplied with hot and cold running water, electric power points for a kettle, the electric drill and the compressor for the airbrush are also needed. However do not despair if you do not have all these requirements; in most cases improvisation is necessary and fortunately chinamending does not necessarily require a lot of room, provided the china to be repaired and the bulk of the materials and tools can be stored safely away, especially from the reach of children. Make sure that you have at least one cupboard that can be kept locked. In mending china one can work in all kinds of nooks and crannies. I know some restorers who work in their kitchens or tucked away in some corner near a large window, using an extended window ledge as a workbench.

The working area will ultimately depend on the individual's circumstances and ingenuity. However, a word about your workbench and stool: it is important to be sure that the height of your bench and stool or chair make for comfortable working. You will be sitting for long periods at a time so be sure you are comfortable and do not have to reach up or bend too far down to your work in an uncomfortable attitude. Resting your feet on a footstool or box is a helpful addition to comfort, and you will find your lap an invaluable extra work surface.

A good strong lamp with flexible arm will be necessary. Never work in a bad light. For matching paints you will need good daylight.

Warning

Many of the materials used in the repair and restoration of china are harmful to the skin; it is therefore advisable to use a good barrier cream before commencing the work. Hydrogen peroxide, Nitromors, ammonia and sodium hydroxide all cause severe burning, so when handling these materials always wear non-slip surgical gloves, and if the chemicals do come in contact with the skin, wash immediately in cold water.

Fabrics and clothing can also suffer irreparable damage from spilt solvents and adhesives, so either wear your oldest clothing or overalls and a good thick apron when working.

When spray painting or using the electric drill, or when working with some solvents and cleaning agents, a respirator and goggles should be worn, as fine spray from the paint and fumes from the solvents can be harmful to the lungs if breathed in. When the drill is used, small hot particles of ceramic fly off at great speed and can cause injury to the skin and eyes, and the very fine particles of dust released into the air should not be inhaled.

The airbrush and the drill should always be operated in a well-ventilated area.

All instructions and warnings which come with the materials should be very carefully read and followed.

Some adhesives and solvents are highly inflammable so care should be taken to keep them well away from open flame. The inflammable nature of these materials should also be borne in mind when

Some of the materials for china mending

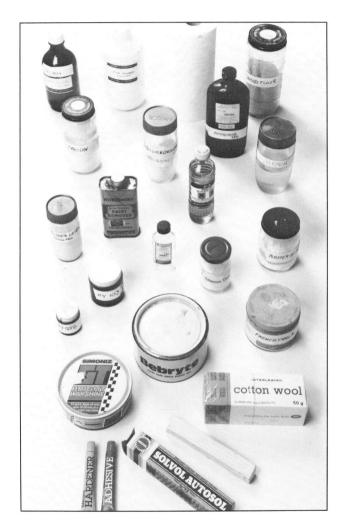

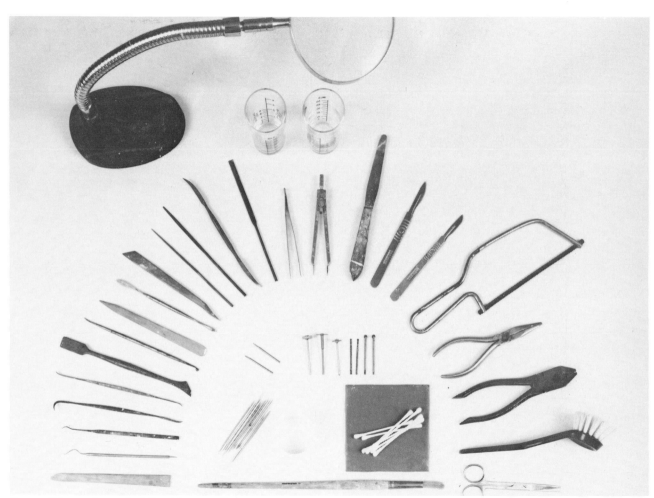

Some of the tools required for china mending

storing them away.

Assemble all tools and equipment and materials for the job ready to commence. It is advisable to buy only the minimum requirement of tools and equipment to begin with; other items can be acquired as they become necessary. The best quality tools should be bought, as the right tools of the best quality go a long way to take the strain out of the work.

Hands, tools, utensils and equipment must always be clinically clean. All bottles, jars of solvents, fillers, adhesives, etc. must be well labelled. Never leave jars and bottles open and replace lids and stoppers immediately after use; apart from the fact that many of the materials have a tendency to evaporate rapidly, even a large and obvious jar can be knocked over quite easily with disastrous results.

Finally, have only one piece of china (i.e. the piece on which you are working) out on the bench at a time. Having several pieces of china scattered about in front of you is courting disaster. One slight movement of the arm can send one of these pieces flying and you will find yourself with a massive and unexpected repair.

---

2. FIRST STEPS

Tools and Equipment Necessary

Tools

Single edge blades *or*
Scalpel handles and blades;
    Swann-Morton handles nos.
    3 and 4, blades nos. 10, 11,
    15, 23
Stainless steel scissors, 10 cm
    (4 in)
Magnifying glass
Pliers, one long-nosed, one
    blunt-nosed
Tweezers, fine-point 13 cm
    (5 in)
Various probes, old dental hand
    tools
Palette knife
Small hacksaw and blades

Materials

Good quality detergent
Synperonic NDB (*Triton X100*)
Nitromors green label, water
    washable (*Methylene chloride*)
Brush to apply Nitromors
Sodium hydroxide, also known
    as caustic soda
Sepiolite (*Magnesium trisilicate*)
Hydrogen peroxide 100 Vol
    (*Hydrogen peroxide 30–35%*)
Ammonia 880 (*Ammonia 28%*)
Distilled water
Acetone
Ferroclene 389 (*Naval jelly*)
Acid resistant brush for use
    with Ferroclene

Household bleach
White spirit (*Mineral spirit,
    Stodard solvent*)
Methylated spirit (*Denatured
    ethyl alcohol*)
Barrier cream

General equipment

White absorbent kitchen paper
Large plastic bowl and soft
    nylon brush
Chinagraph pencil (*Volatile
    crayon*)
Waterproof labels
Notebook and pen
Apron
Non-slip surgical gloves
Cotton wool

Cleaning

When choosing your first piece of china to repair, aim for simple breaks. A cup, saucer or bowl broken in a maximum of three pieces is ideal. Start on a piece which is highly decorated, as coloured pieces with a good deal of pattern are much easier to repair than plain china.

Before starting to work on any piece, it is important to make sure that your hands, the equipment you are using and the broken pieces of china are all spotlessly clean. Dirty broken edges and those which still have bits of adhesive on them will never bond successfuly: even the tiniest speck of dirt or old adhesive will prevent the perfect join. Therefore, begin by washing every piece you receive very thoroughly in warm water and soap. A good household detergent is quite adequate for this purpose. Synperonic NDB *(Triton X100)* is a good non-ionic detergent for cleaning ceramics. It is used in water in concentrations of up to 1%. At this stage it is not necessary to use the de-ionized water or distilled water mentioned later in the chapter. If the pieces are highly decorated with delicate moulding and embellishments, brush carefully with a soft nylon brush, taking care not to damage the raised decorations. Do not dry with a towel or the absorbent kitchen paper as bits of fluff and fabric will get caught up on the sharp edges of the decorations and will be difficult to move; they can also pull and break off little chips from the decorations. Stand the piece on a clean cloth in a warm dry place to drain or, if a more speedy process is desired, play warm air from a hairdryer over the piece to dry off any excess moisture.

For this first stage of washing, tap water and household detergent are used; in all subsequent washing and rinsing and in the mixing up of pastes and bleaching solutions, de-ionized or distilled water should be used. A de-ionizing unit is required for this purpose, but this is an expensive piece of equipment, and distilled water, such as that used in car batteries and steam irons, can be used equally effectively. Tap water may be used on unimportant pieces of domestic china.

The restorer will frequently be presented with ceramics which have previously been glued together, perhaps several years ago, with one of a great variety of glues. It will be necessary to break down these old repairs first. Fortunately the great majority of these joins will separate when the piece is placed in a bowl of very hot water and allowed to soak for several minutes. Never pour boiling water on to the china, but place the piece in hot water gently bringing the temperature up by gradually adding more and more very hot water, until it is almost at boiling point.

There are, however, always the more stubborn joins, and it is here that the restorer's job can become somewhat nerve-racking. When the piece is still warm, gently exert a little pressure and try to coax the piece apart. Do not exert too much pressure as you could find yourself with a multiple break on your hands. If the join still refuses to part, soak the piece in water then dip a brush into a small quantity of Nitromors (*methylene chloride*) and apply it to the joins. It is important to soak the piece in water before applying the Nitromors, as the water acts as a barrier, preventing the Nitromors and old adhesive from being drawn down into the body of the porcelain and thereby causing a stain. Leave the pieces for about twenty minutes then gently flex the pieces to try and separate them. If they do not part, repeat the process and leave for one or two hours. Nitromors can be left on a join for 24 hours or longer, but never let it dry on the join and always check at intervals. Warm water poured over the join after the Nitromors has been applied can accelerate the dismantling process. Nitromors can cause burning to the skin so it is advisable to wear gloves and to work with care.

Having parted the old repair, examine the broken edges carefully through a magnifying glass. This will usually reveal specks of old adhesive and dirt not always visible to the naked eye. Most glues will come away quite easily, but some will still adhere, usually in corners and crevices. Gently scrape these out with a blade, taking care not to dislodge bits of ceramic. Brushing with a soft nylon brush is also helpful in removing bits of old adhesive and dirt. When you are quite satisfied that *all* the old glue has been removed, wash the pieces

again in warm water and detergent, brushing each piece gently with a soft nylon brush. Always wash the pieces in a bowl and not over a sink. Rinse and dry thoroughly.

Rivets

In the early days, restorers used rivets to give their bonded pieces additional strength. These are little bolts made of metal or thick wire cemented into small holes drilled on either side of the break edge of the piece. The wire was snapped into the holes rather like staples are clipped into bundles of paper. The rivets then secured the two broken pieces firmly together. These metal 'staples' marching across an otherwise attractive piece of ceramic are most unsightly, but at least they have held the broken bits together and preserved them for us, so that we today, with our new techniques and materials, can restore them to a greater perfection.

To remove a rivet, soak the piece in very hot water to soften the cement surrounding the rivet; then, using a pointed probing instrument, pick out all the cement in the rivet hole. This usually leaves the rivet quite loose and it can be lifted out with a pair of pointed tweezers without much effort. If, however, it stays firm after you have dug out the cement, grip the rivet with a pair of pointed pliers, and rock it gently back and forth to loosen it. Some restorers recommend sliding a thin blade or probe under the rivet and gently forcing it up to dislodge it; with this method care must be taken to avoid damaging the glaze on the porcelain. Stubborn thick rivets which will not come away with the pliers have to be removed by sawing through the metal with a fine hacksaw blade. Again, watch to see that you do not saw on to the surface of the porcelain and so damage the glaze. When you have sawn through the metal, gently pull each end of the rivet up with your pliers. Make sure every bit of cement is removed from the rivet holes. A little Nitromors and warm water often helps to soften and dislodge the remaining cement.

It is important that the rivet holes should be quite free of all old cement and stains before re-filling them. If it is difficult to dislodge the old cement with the pointed probing instrument by hand you may have to drill these stubborn old bits of filling away with an electric drill and diamond-pointed drill head (see page 40 for instructions on using the drill).

Stains

Some stains found in ceramics can be very difficult to move and time, perseverance and patience are essential ingredients for this operation.

It is possible to remove minor stains by soaking the piece in a solution of household bleach and water in the proportion of one part of bleach to four of water. This solution can be strengthened to one part bleach to one part water, but this should be done gradually and pieces should not be left soaking in the bleaching solution for long periods as it can damage the glaze. In all cases where there is gold decoration on the porcelain, care must be taken and constant checking is advisable to ensure that the gold does not get drawn into the body of the porcelain causing a very ugly purple stain. If the bleaching solution fails to remove the stain a second method can be tried. Here the ceramic is soaked in a solution of sodium hydroxide and water. Follow the instructions on the label and always add the powder to the water. Wear gloves when handling sodium hydroxide as it can cause bad skin irritation. If it comes in contact with the skin wash immediately in cold water.

Fill a plastic bowl with cold water. You will need a big bowl and plenty of water, if the piece to be repaired is a large one. Add sodium hydroxide in proportion to the amount of water used (usually 1 part of sodium hydroxide to 5 of water). Stir well with a wooden spoon. Immerse the piece in the solution and leave for about twenty minutes. Keep checking to ensure that some reaction is taking place. If not, add a little more sodium hydroxide to the water. It may be necessary to leave the porcelain soaking for several hours, as much as 24 hours or even longer, but never let the sodium hydroxide solution dry out on the piece.

This method is very good for removing dirt from cracks and cleans porcelain very efficiently. Constant checking is important especially at the beginning and also when there is any gold decoration. Metal handles and decorations must be kept clear of this solution. If a piece has metal embellishments it must not be soaked, but strips of cotton wool should be soaked in the solution and then placed over the stained area. Do not let the cotton wool dry out, and change it frequently. Once all the stains and dirt have disappeared rinse the piece very thoroughly in cold water and dry.

The use of Sepiolite (*Magnesium trisilicate*) is a third method for removing stains and is most effective in the removal of stains from pottery, marble and stoneware. Mix the Sepiolite with distilled water to the consistency of paste. The piece is first soaked in water and then the paste is applied with a palette knife to cover the entire area to a depth of 25 mm (1 inch). It is then left to dry for 24 hours, during which time the stain is drawn up into the paste. When the paste is partially dry, it starts to crack. At this stage it should be carefully picked off and brushed off a little at a time and then washed

down. It may be necessary to repeat this process several times before the stain has been completely removed. If the stains are greasy or oily, the paste should be made up of Sepiolite and white spirit in place of water and before using the Sepiolite the piece should be degreased by wiping with Nitromors or acetone.

Hydrogen peroxide 100 Vol (*hydrogen peroxide 30-35%*), one part to three parts water, to which is added a few drops of ammonia 880 (*ammonia 28%*), is an effective method for removing stubborn stains and is recommended by the Victoria and Albert Museum. Again it is important to pre-soak the piece in water, especially in the case of earthenware and pottery. Pieces of cotton wool are then soaked in the hydrogen peroxide solution, lifted up and out of the solution by means of a pair of tweezers (it is advisable to wear gloves when working with this solution for it causes bad burning) and the cotton wool is patted on to the stained areas on the ceramic. Do not leave these swabs to dry out on the ceramic. The piece should be placed in a covered container to prevent the swabs from drying out too rapidly. Change the swabs frequently (about every 2 to 3 hours) always rinsing the ceramic thoroughly before applying fresh swabs. Care must be taken when using this solution and a constant check should be made on how the solution is reacting on the ceramic in the early stages. This treatment may have to go on for as long as two or three weeks in the case of very stubborn stains, until all traces of the stain have disappeared. When the ceramic needs more than 12 hours treatment, soak it overnight in water, applying the fresh swabs the following day. This method is very effective in removing stains left by rivets.

Ferroclene 389 (*Naval jelly*), a phosphoric acid liquid, is a very useful stain remover especially for removing rust stains. The stains are removed by dabbing cotton wool dipped in a solution of one part Ferroclene to two parts water, and then placing it on to the stain. An acid-resistant brush is most useful for applying Ferroclene. Rinse very thoroughly in water, and finally wipe with methylated spirits (*denatured ethyl alcohol*).

Rinse all objects very thoroughly after treatment with any of the stain removal materials and solutions and leave to dry thoroughly.

For newly-broken pieces a silk rag dipped in acetone and wiped over the break edges is all that is necessary.

There are some occasions when a stain will not budge and it is at this point that defeat has to be conceded. If the repair is being done for a client, it is advisable to get in touch with him and explain the situation before proceeding with the repair. Make notes on the type of ceramic, type of stain, method used, results, problems encountered and how these were dealt with and overcome. This will prove to be a very helpful reference for subsequent work.

3. BONDING

Tools and Equipment Necessary

Tools
Spatula
Magnifying glass
Stainless steel scissors, 10 cm
  (4 in)
Various probes, old dental hand
  tools

Materials
Araldite epoxy resin, 2-tube
  pack, not rapid (*Devcon Clear*)
Araldite AY103 with hardener
  HY956 (*Epotek 301 and
  hardener or RP103 and
  hardener H956*)
Cyanoacrylate resin adhesive,
  Loctite IS496 (*Eastman 910 or
  Permabond*)

Sintolit (*Pliacre*)
Polyvinyl acetate emulsion,
  Vinamul 6815 (*Jade 403*)
Titanium dioxide
White modelling putty,
  Plasticine (*Plastelina Roma
  Italian No. 2 white*)
Methylated spirit (*Denatured
  ethyl alcohol*)
Acetone
Distilled water
French chalk or talc

General equipment
Mixing tiles
Transparent adhesive tape,
  Sellotape (*Scotchtape*)
Tape dispenser

Clean cloths and rags
White absorbent kitchen paper
Sandbox containing silver sand
  61 × 36 × 16 cm
  (24 × 14 × 6 in)
Apron
Wooden cocktail sticks
Chinagraph pencil (*Volatile
  crayon*)
Notebook and pen
Waterproof labels
Plate racks
Sand bags

Do resist the impulse to reach for the adhesive and stick the bits together immediately you receive them. You should first tape the pieces together without the application of the adhesive. By doing this dry run as it is called, you will be able to decide how best to fit the pieces together to make the perfect union. Imperfections and problems will then become apparent without the additional job of having to wipe away the adhesive and start again. You must, however, avoid grating the edges together during this operation, as bits will tend to crumble away and this will impede a perfect bond.

Another advantage of the dry run is that you will be able to decide the best way to support the piece after bonding. These early steps must be done to perfection for a bad bond will *never* be concealed by filling and over painting. By putting the pieces together first without the adhesive you will get used to the 'feel' of the pieces you are working with and the later stages will then seem to follow on more easily.

Remember to make sure that your hands, tools, equipment and the fragments on which you are working are all spotlessly clean before you start, and throughout the process keep your hands clean and dusted with French chalk or talc.

Supporting the bonded pieces

You should always try to make full use of gravitational pull when setting bonded pieces up for drying. Carefully examine the pieces and position them at such an angle that the upper piece will be supported squarely on and pressing down upon the lower piece. During the drying time this upper piece will bear down and a closer join will be the result. It is important to be sure that the pieces are fitting together at the correct angle and not tilting forwards or backwards. A help in supporting pieces balanced in this way is a sandbox. This is a box preferably of metal or plastic, approximately $61 \times 36 \times 16$ cm ($24 \times 14 \times 6$ in) filled to a depth of about $7\frac{1}{2}$ to 10 cm (3 to 4 in) with silver sand. Small plates and dishes can be supported in plate racks, the angle being adjusted with little wedges of modelling putty. Little linen or canvas bags of various sizes filled with sand are also very useful for supporting bonded pieces. Quite an effective means of supporting a bonded plate is to place it

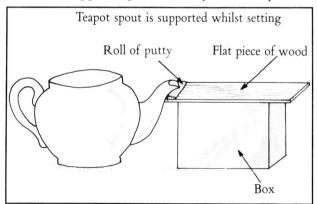

Teapot spout is supported whilst setting

Roll of putty   Flat piece of wood

Box

vertically in a drawer and close the drawer gently on to it to hold it steady.

Pads of modelling putty placed on either side of a cup can hold it steady and prevent it from rolling over when setting a cup handle or during the operation of bonding a handle on to a cup.

All sorts of bits and pieces about the house come in useful as supports and you must always work out your method of support and have it ready prepared *before* you start bonding. You will find yourself resorting again and again to your own ingenuity when working out the different means of supporting the bonded pieces.

Be very gentle when removing the adhesive tape from the ceramic after the dry run. If the tape is ripped off, broken chips of ceramic and gilding can be inadvertently removed.

With a clean tile before you, adhesive tape to hand, preferably in a dispenser so that it can be easily broken off, or with strips cut off and placed so that they are readily available, and with very clean hands, squeeze equal portions of Araldite (*Devcon Clear*) from each tube in the two-tube pack on to the tile and mix together very thoroughly with a spatula or small knife.

A tiny speck of titanium dioxide can be added to the mixture to keep the adhesive white. Only the minutest speck is needed as you do not want to weaken the adhesive quality with the addition of too much titanium dioxide powder.

In cold weather the tubes can be warmed by putting them into a small container of hot water, but wipe them well before squeezing adhesive on to the tile.

The china to be bonded should also be slightly warm and this can be done by placing it next to a radiator for a few minutes. The broken edges must be quite dry.

Take a small strip of adhesive tape and stick it on

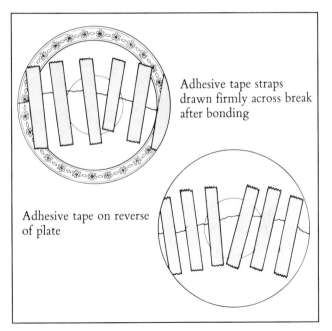

Adhesive tape straps drawn firmly across break after bonding

Adhesive tape on reverse of plate

to the china at right angles to the break edge so that half of the tape overlaps the edge; this half must then be folded back from the edge. More pieces are placed at approximately $2\frac{1}{2}$ cm (1 in) intervals at right angles across the break, in the same way. Place corresponding strips of tape on the reverse side. The width between the strips will, of course, depend on the size of the repair.

Pick up the mixed-up adhesive on the tip of a wooden cocktail stick or a metal spatula so that a fine thread hangs down from the stick and place this thread carefully down the centre of the broken edge of the warmed china. Beginners tend to spread the adhesive too thickly. A good guideline to follow is the feeling that you are using too little adhesive. It is not necessary to put the adhesive on the break edges of both broken pieces. Bring the two pieces together. Bring the folded pieces of adhesive tape up and press them down across the join. Repeat this with the corresponding pieces of tape on the reverse side. Additional pieces of tape can be added later. When you are satisfied that the

Top: Equal quantities of Araldite squeezed on to a clean tile and thoroughly mixed together with a very small quantity of titanium dioxide

Bottom: Applying mixed adhesive to break edge of plate with spatula

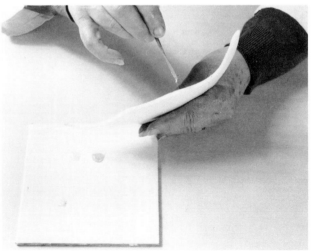

two pieces of broken china are joined together as perfectly as possible, exert some pressure on the two pieces and start lifting the strips of tape and pulling them tightly across the join. Repeat this process with all the tapes. To test if the join is correctly aligned, run your finger nail or a blade or a sharp pointed instrument across the join. If there is a slight ridge, correct it by a little pressure or movement of the pieces. It is important to pull each piece of adhesive tape with equal pressure across the join. Excess adhesive will be squeezed out of the join and the bond tightened. The excess adhesive can be removed with a sharp blade or a brush moistened in methylated spirits. Do not have too much meths on the brush; it will dilute the adhesive and weaken the bond if it flows into the join. Pieces with gold decoration need extra care and must be cleaned with methylated spirit before the adhesive has set. Unglazed pottery should also be cleaned of adhesive at once. On other pieces hardened adhesive can be removed gently by lifting it off carefully with a sharp blade or rubbing down with fine abrasive paper.

Avoid handling the join too much as no matter how clean you keep your hands the natural grease from the fingers can discolour the joins. Sticky fingers pick up particles of dust and dirt and in no time at all you will find yourself with a very messy piece of work which will have to be broken down, cleaned and re-glued. Therefore constant washing and dusting of the hands with French chalk or talc is important and, in the end, time-saving.

Place bonded objects, well strapped, into a sandbox, drawer, or suitable support and leave to set.

Araldite sets in approximately 12 hours at 16°C (60°F). The warmth of the room will affect setting times. After one hour you can check on your repair and it may be necessary to adjust it a fraction. A little pressure or extra pulling on the tapes can be done at this juncture.

A stronger join and accelerated curing time is achieved by heating. A piece heated at 150°C (300°F) will have set in 30 minutes. But heating ceramics is a risky business as some pieces can crack and discolour with stoving. The slower room temperature method of curing is recommended.

Multiple breaks

When a piece of china is broken into more than two fragments, the term applied to the broken piece is multiple break or multi-break. In the case of multi-breaks you will have to decide on the order in which you intend to reassemble the pieces. It is not a bad idea to treat the operation rather like a jigsaw puzzle first laying out the pieces on a clean sheet of paper, then commencing a dry run, slowly

Left: Vase broken into sixteen pieces

Above: Vase bonded and cracks, chips and missing pieces filled with composition

Right: The restored vase

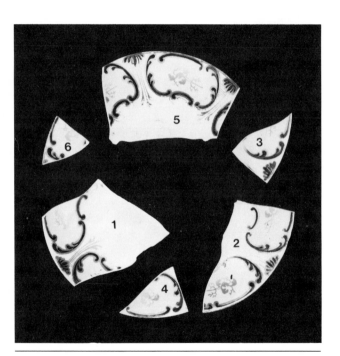

Saucer broken into six pieces

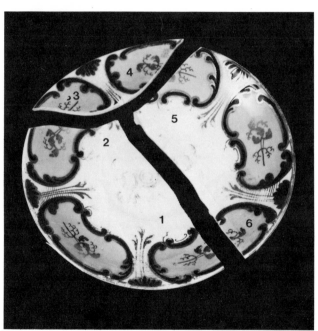

The correct sequence of assembly. The next step would be to bond 5/6 to 1/2 with 3/4 making the final join

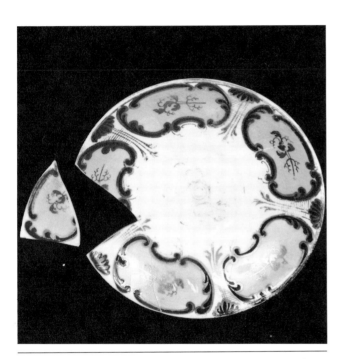

Saucer incorrectly assembled showing how a piece can be locked out

The restored saucer

building up the pieces, strapping the bits together as you go along, without the use of adhesive. It is advisable to start with the largest piece and build up from this foundation, numbering the pieces as you proceed either with a chinagraph pencil (*volatile crayon*) or by printing numbers on small waterproof labels and sticking these to each piece as you work. Numbers can also be printed on small pieces of gum strip and stuck on to each piece. Gum strip can be removed later with water or acetone.

It is not usually possible to put a multi-break together in one go as you cannot expect un-set pieces to stay in place when you are exerting pressure on the other pieces.

In many cases it is more satisfactory to stick two small pieces together before fitting them into a wider area or to bond several pieces into separate units and then finally fit the bonded units together. It is important to follow the order you established in the dry run to avoid locking out. This happens when the pieces are assembled in the wrong order so that a piece cannot be fitted in place without dislodging the surrounding pieces. When bonding a multiple break, do not take the adhesive to the end of each break edge, but stop just a fraction short of the end or the adhesive will extend on to the adjoining break edge and will inhibit the next join.

On very rare occasions it is advantageous to bond the piece in one session and only by doing the dry run can you decide which course to take.

Always keep the adhesive as thin as possible, for the cumulative bulk of adhesive on each broken bit, as you build the pieces up, can put the pieces out of alignment and you will have difficulty fitting in the final piece.

Strapping the pieces firmly and pulling the tapes lightly but firmly across the join help to make a good union between the pieces.

In small breaks, e.g. cup handles, where strapping is not possible, a pad of modelling putty can be used to imbed one piece, while the other piece is held in position by another pad of putty. Care, however, must be taken to keep the putty out of the break.

A dowel will help to hold two awkward pieces together. This will be described in chapter 4.

Top left: Ironstone bowl broken into seven pieces

Bottom left: Bowl strapped together in a dry run showing missing pieces

Top right: Bowl bonded with chips and cracks filled

Bottom right: Bowl completed. It was decided not to make an invisible repair as the bowl had warped

29

When the handle or shank of a ladle has snapped, it can be quite difficult to support the pieces for a successful union. The bowl of the ladle should be imbedded in a mould made of modelling putty and the handle supported by two pads of putty, as it is not always possible to strap these difficult pieces. A quick setting resin, e.g. cyanoacrylate adhesive, Loctite IS496 (*Eastman 910 or Permabond*), is useful for bonding small pieces which cannot be taped. It is very fast curing and bonds glass and smooth break edges in seconds. There is therefore very little time for adjusting the fit once the adhesive has been applied. Practise fitting the pieces together before applying the adhesive, and when you are quite sure you can bring the pieces together in correct alignment, put a small drop of adhesive on to one edge, bring the two pieces together and press firmly for about 10 seconds. Not as simple as it sounds; it is surprisingly difficult to hold an object steady for 10 seconds.

Sintolit is a polyester resin which sets in the slightly longer time of 10 minutes giving one a little more leeway for adjustment. For use, 2% to 3% hardener is mixed with the resin i.e. 1 to $1\frac{1}{2}$ parts hardener to 50 parts Sintolit, a small amount applied to one break edge and the pieces are brought together and supported for 10 minutes while setting. The addition of titanium dioxide and kaolin makes a good quick-setting filler. Sin-

tolit is also good for bonding earthenware and ceramics which have a porous body. It is strong and its viscosity prevents it from being drawn into the porous body of the earthenware or pottery, and avoids the possibility of staining. It is not recommended to heat ceramics when using either cyanoacrylate adhesive or Sintolit as cyanoacrylate adhesive will lose its strength at $120°C$ ($248°F$) and will melt at $168°C$ ($334°F$) and Sintolit will melt at $100°C$ ($212°F$).

These fast setting adhesives are not as reliable as Araldite and should only be used on cabinet pieces when the strength of the join is not so important.

Araldite AY103 and HY956 (*Epotek 301 or RP103*). AY103 is a plasticised liquid epoxy resin which when mixed with the hardener HY956 produces a more liquid adhesive than the two-tube variety. It is therefore very useful when bonding cracks and warped pieces. Mix AY103 and HY956 in the proportion of one part HY956 to five parts AY103, stir thoroughly and leave for 20 minutes in a covered container before using. (For Epotek 301 plus hardener or RP103 plus hardener H956, mix 4 parts resin to 1 part hardener.) A very small amount of titanium dioxide mixed into the adhesive will prevent it from yellowing. Bonds that have been set with this resin can be broken down with the solvent De-Solv 292.

AY103 with HY956 cures in approximately 24

hours at 20°C (68°F) in 3 hours at 60°C (140°F) or in 20 minutes at 100°C (212°F).

Polyvinyl acetate emulsion, Vinamul 6815 (*Jade 403*) is the most suitable adhesive for pottery and earthenware as it does not get drawn into the porous body of the ceramic. The broken edges of the piece should be absolutely clean. It is very important to damp both edges thoroughly with distilled water before applying the adhesive. Apply to one edge only, then bring the broken edges together and strap in the usual way.

Warped or 'sprung' pieces

Quite frequently the problem of warped pieces

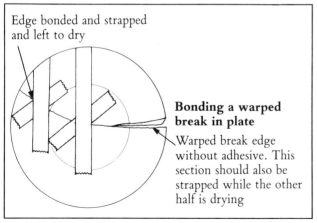

Edge bonded and strapped and left to dry

Bonding a warped break in plate

Warped break edge without adhesive. This section should also be strapped while the other half is drying

will occur. When a ceramic breaks, the tension is released on the piece and often one or more of the broken fragments become distorted. It is very difficult to get a perfect union again when reassembling the warped pieces. It is not always possible to deal successfully with this problem and there are times when one simply has to make the join as near as possible, but it will not be a perfect bond. At other times, with really badly sprung pieces, one may decide that repair is impossible.

The method for dealing with warped pieces is as follows:

1. Apply adhesive to half the length of the break only.
2. Strap the whole length of the break (this includes the half without the adhesive).
3. Keep checking the join to make sure that the bonded half is adhering tightly and not slipping out of alignment. Leave to set. In this case the setting time should be at least two or three days to be absolutely sure the first half of the break is well and truly bonded.
4. Remove the tape and gently squeeze more adhesive into the unbonded half, warming the piece if necessary.
5. Gently coax the sprung end into position exerting some pressure, and at the same time pulling a piece of tape across the break to fasten the two halves together.

6. Pull straps tightly across the break with equal tension on the front and on the reverse sides. Care must be taken in exerting pressure on the warped pieces as breaks can occur so easily when trying to force an alignment,
7. Leave to set, suitably supported.

Cracked pieces

A piece which has a crack extending only about three-quarters of the way across and which appears to remain strong without any flexing movement is best left alone. Simply soak the piece in a bleaching solution or a solution of sodium hydroxide and water, to remove the deeply engrained dirt and dust which probably make the crack unsightly. Do not try to bond the crack.

When, however, the crack stretches the full length of the piece, so that it flexes with pressure, the piece should be well washed so that all dirt is removed. Then warm it and insert a fine blade gently into the crack to open it a fraction, meanwhile forcing a thin trickle of adhesive into the crack. Then remove the blade and strap the crack up firmly. In most cases it is simpler to break the piece and rebond it.

Do not forget to take notes of the methods used to break down the old repair, solvents used for the

removal of stains, types of adhesive used in bonding, the problems encountered, etc. Practise bonding on old kitchen pieces, but always aim at the perfect union, for acquiring proficiency in these early stages is most important. Joins that are even slightly out of alignment will be impossible to disguise with filling and painting, but will become more obvious with each subsequent step.

Left: Bowl broken into eight pieces

Above: Bowl strapped together in a dry run

Top right: Bowl bonded with cracks and chips filled

Below right: The restored bowl

—4. FILLINGS, REINFORCING AND— RUBBING DOWN

Tools, materials and equipment necessary

Tools
Spatula
Wire cutters
Stainless steel scissors, 10 cm
  (4 in)
Palette knife
Boxwood modelling tools
Various probes, old dental hand
  tools
Scalpel handles and blades;
  Swann-Morton handles nos. 3
  and 4, blades nos. 10, 11, 15,
  23
Magnifying glass
Electric drill with diamond drill
  head and discs

Materials
Araldite epoxy resin, 2-tube
  pack (*Devcon Clear*)

Araldite AY103 with hardener
  HY956 (*Epotek 301 and
  hardener or RP103 and hardener
  H956*)
Sylmasta 2-pack (*Elmer's epoxy
  resin*)
Filler powders: Dental plaster,
  fine grade or plaster of Paris
  (*Hydrocal*)
  Kaolin
  Marble flour (*marble powder*)
  Polyfilla, interior
  Polyfilla, fine-surface, ready-
  mixed (*Polyfix*)
Titanium dioxide
White modelling putty,
  Plasticine (*Plastelina Roma
  Italian No. 2 white*)
Brass dowelling wire, 16, 18, 19
  gauge

Stainless steel dowelling wire
Solvol Autosol polish
Abrasive papers, wet and dry
  320–1000/1200; Flex-I-Grit
  400/600
Methylated spirit (*Denatured
  ethyl alcohol*)
French chalk or talc

General equipment
Mixing tiles and saucers
Transparent adhesive tape,
  Sellotape (*Scotchtape*)
Tape dispenser
Clean cloths and rags
White absorbent kitchen paper
Sandbox containing silver sand,
  61 × 36 × 16 cm (24 × 14 × 6 in)
Graded medicine glass
Wooden cocktail sticks

It is very rare that a piece of broken china will only require bonding; almost every piece will have a small chip missing, or a minute hole or crack will have to be filled in. When a piece is broken, bits invariably crumble away and when the broken pieces are fitted together there are nearly always small gaps here and there.

There is a fairly wide choice of filling material and you should experiment with them all and then choose the type of filler with which you are happiest and also the one most suitable for the type of ceramic to be filled. The first three are suitable for all ceramics.

Fillers

Sylmasta (*Elmer's Epoxy Resin*)

This can be bought ready made up. It comes in two tins or packs, and all that is necessary is to mix equal amounts from each tin or pack very thoroughly together, kneading it until the creamy colour of the catalyst and the white colour of the resin are thoroughly blended. Unmixed, the components have an almost indefinite shelf life. Mixed, the filler remains workable for up to two hours and can be moulded, shaped and smoothed during that period. Full setting strength is achieved in approximately 24 hours at room temperature. Setting times can be accelerated if heat is applied but do not heat above 100°C (212°F).

Two-tube Araldite (*Devcon Clear*) and titanium dioxide

Equal portions from each tube are mixed together very thoroughly with the addition of titanium dioxide powder. A tremendous amount of titanium dioxide is required for fillings. Continue mixing in more and more titanium dioxide until the mixture can be handled without it sticking to the fingers, and can be rolled out like pastry. This type of filling is very white and strong.

Good fine dental plaster or plaster of Paris (*hydrocal*) can be added in place of the vast quantity of titanium dioxide to make up a very strong, white composition. In this case squeeze out equal portions of Araldite from each tube on to a clean tile. Mix the resin and the hardener very thoroughly together, add a small portion of titanium dioxide in order to keep the composition white, then proceed to mix in dental plaster or plaster of Paris. Mix all these components together very thoroughly with a spatula or small flat knife until the mixture is firm and stiff enough to be rolled out like pastry and does not stick to your fingers. Keep dusting your hands with French chalk as this helps to keep the composition from sticking and also keeps the hands clean and free of grease.

AY103/HY956 Araldite resin with hardener
(Epotek 301 and hardener or RP103 and H956)
This is a more liquid form of the two-tube Araldite. Using a graded medicine glass or small container, pour 5 parts AY103 into the glass. Add 1 part HY956 and stir very well, mixing the two parts together very thoroughly. (For Epotek 301 or RP103 mix 4 parts resin to 1 part hardener). If a smaller quantity is required, drip 5 drops of AY103 on to a clean tile or mixing saucer from a cocktail stick or metal measuring rod. Clean the rod or stick, dip it into the HY956 and add one drop to the AY103 in the mixing saucer. Mix together thoroughly. Cover this mixture and leave it to stand for 15 to 20 minutes. Do not stand the container on hot pipes or warming plates as heat accelerates the curing time of this adhesive. After 20 minutes, a small amount of titanium dioxide can be added to the mixture to retard any tendency for it to yellow. Plaster of Paris or kaolin can be added, as with the two-tube variety. When mixed thoroughly together a good composition is achieved for filling.

AY103/HY956 has a usable life of approximately 45 to 60 minutes when mixed up into the quantity of 50 grammes ($1\frac{3}{4}$ oz). It is not advisable to mix up large quantities as this mixture can generate a good deal of heat when curing. If a sizeable amount has to be made, it is a good idea to divide the mixture into several containers, so that it does not stand in one compact mass, and the rise in temperature and consequent shortening of its usable life is prevented. Always aim to mix up only the quantity necessary for immediate use.

HY956 is hygroscopic and will absorb moisture when exposed to humid atmospheric conditions. It is therefore most important to keep the mixture covered during the curing times.

Curing times for AY103/HY956 are as follows:

20 minutes at 100°C (212°F)
3 hours at 60°C (140°F)
8 to 12 hours at 40°C (104°F)
24 hours at 20°C (68°F)

The shelf life of AY103 is five years and HY956 is 3 years. Always store in a cool dry place and keep both the resin and the hardener firmly sealed.

Care should be taken in handling the resin and hardener. Although generally harmless, they can affect some sensitive skins. Barrier creams, rubber gloves and always washing hands after working with these substances are all advisable precautions. Kerodex 71 is a good barrier cream and Kerocleanse 22 is a recommended resin-removing cream. Make sure your working area is well ventilated and do not allow the uncured materials to come into contact with food or cooking utensils. Read and follow all instructions that come with the materials.

Kaolin mixed into Araldite (either two-tube Araldite or the AY103/HY956 mixture) imparts a pale ivory colour to the mixture. Pigment powder colours can be mixed with the filler powders to match the ground colour of the porcelain, but it is not easy to get a very good match as the colours usually darken with the introduction of the plaster of Paris or kaolin. However a good toning match can be achieved with practice and experience.

Clean all utensils with methylated spirits (*denatured ethyl alcohol*).

Polyfilla Interior
Add the powder to water and mix to a stiff workable putty-like consistency. This makes a most suitable filling for pottery. It can be built up in layers and easily smoothed down by dipping a finger, modelling tool or rag in water and smoothing over the surface of the filling when it is partially set. It rubs down easily and an excellent finish can be obtained with a final application of ready mixed Fine Surface Polyfilla (Polyfix). This mixture comes ready made up in packs and can be bought at most hardware shops. Smooth the mixture over the Polyfilla filling and leave to dry. Do not apply the Fine Surface Polyfilla until the original Polyfilla filling has dried. A final rubbing down with a fine abrasive paper will leave a satin smooth finish.

Filling in cracks

After a piece of china has been bonded and it has set and is completely dry, examine the bond very carefully through a magnifying glass. If the join needs filling, and it usually does, mix up a putty filler composition, as described above, suitable for the type of porcelain being repaired. The composition should be slightly thinner for cracks than for filling larger areas. Now take up a small amount of putty on the end of a spatula or modelling tool and smear it *across* the crack, pressing the mixture down quite firmly and working it into the join. Clean the tool and dip it in methylated spirits (*denatured ethyl alcohol*). It should be just moist, not dripping wet. Now run the moist flat end of the spatula or tool *along* the line of the join, smoothing and filling and working it into the crack as the spatula travels up along the join. Leave to dry. When the filling is almost dry any excess can be cut off with a sharp blade dipped in French chalk or meths. Do not try to cut the excess putty or filling away when it is still wet as you will drag the filling up out of the crack. The filling process may have to be repeated if some little gaps have been missed in the first application. When quite dry, rub down with abrasive paper, taking care not to damage the surrounding glaze. Use wet and dry abrasive paper,

620 to start with, graduating to a finer paper, such as wet and dry 1000 to 1200, to finish off so as to get a fine smooth finish ready for painting. Detailed notes on rubbing down can be found at the end of this section.

Chips

When small chips are missing from the edges and rims of ceramics, the filling will need to be supported during the drying, as the putty has a tendency to sag. Two or three layers of adhesive tape stretched across the missing area will be sufficient to support small chips. Modelling putty can also be used as a support. It should be rolled out flat and smooth, slightly larger than the missing area. Dust the putty with French chalk so that the filling does not stick to it. Then strap the putty on to the piece so that it overlaps the sides of the missing area; do not allow the putty to get on to the break edges. Mix up some composition a little thicker than that used for filling cracks. Apply a very thin smear of adhesive to the break edge and press a small amount of filling firmly against the break edges, making sure that no air is trapped between the broken edges and the filling. Pack the filling completely into the missing area. Smooth the surface of the filling with a tool dipped in meths. When the surface is partially dry dip your finger or a tool in meths, so that it is just moist, and rub over the filling to smooth it down to a good finish, and thereby avoid excessive sanding down later. If the missing chip is large, you will have to build up the filling in layers, allowing each layer to dry before adding the next one. You need not be too particular about the first layers being smooth; a slightly rough surface acts as a good key for the next layer. Always slightly overfill on the final layer.

Composition heats while curing and drying. If air has been trapped under the filling, when it has dried small holes will appear on the surface of the filling. These tiny holes are not easy to fill in, so open them up with a sharp pointed instrument before applying more filler. Very large chips and supports will be dealt with in the section on moulds and casts, chapter 6.

Shell breaks

These are small slivers of porcelain broken off from the edge of plates and rims of cups, bowls, etc., leaving an area scooped out in the shape of a shell, hence the name. As this repair is not always as simple as it first appears, a good strong adhesive putty is recommended, but for shallower chips and very small holes the composition will have to be made softer. The surface of the break should first be smeared with a very thin layer of adhesive to ensure that the filler will adhere well, When the shell break is small, mix up the composition and fill the broken area in one go, pressing the filling into the area and pushing it down firmly against the sides. It is important to press and spread the filling firmly into the break, to avoid air being trapped under the composition and causing little holes to appear on the surface of the filling when it has dried. Overfill the area by a very small amount to avoid having to mix up more composition and apply it to the first layer after it has dried and been rubbed down. The filling should extend just the smallest fraction over the sides of the break on to the unbroken surface. When it is almost set, but still able to be smoothed, dip a suitable tool, a spatula or modelling tool, into meths. Shake off excess moisture, leaving the tool just wet but not dripping, and smooth it over the surface. Then leave to dry with the filling standing just a little proud of the surrounding area.

When the shell break is large and deep, spread a thin layer of epoxy resin over the broken area and build up the missing area in very thin layers of composition, making sure that the final layer is pressed down and spread firmly. Make sure that air is not trapped beneath the filling by spreading the layers thinly and applying the composition smoothly and firmly over the entire area. Each layer must be allowed to dry before the next layer is applied. Extend the filling a fraction over on to the unbroken surface. When the filling is partially dry, dip a spatula into meths, shake off excess moisture and smooth over surface. Leave to dry and when quite set rub surface down with wet and dry abrasive paper until flush and smooth with the surrounding area.

With all fillings, cracks, chips, shell breaks, etc. there must not be the slightest gap between the area that has been filled and the unbroken area.

Rivet holes

When rivets have been removed from ceramics, the holes will have to be filled in. Take a small quantity of filling composition, mixed up to a slightly softer consistency than for chips and larger fillings, and start to pack it into the holes, a small amount at a time, pressing it firmly against the bottom and sides of the holes. Again, as with all fillings, care must be taken to avoid trapping air beneath the filling. Push in small quantities at a time until the hole is completely filled. Slightly overfill the hole so that the filling stands a little above the surrounding area. If the rivet hole goes right through the porcelain, stick a little adhesive tape across one side, so that your filling does not go

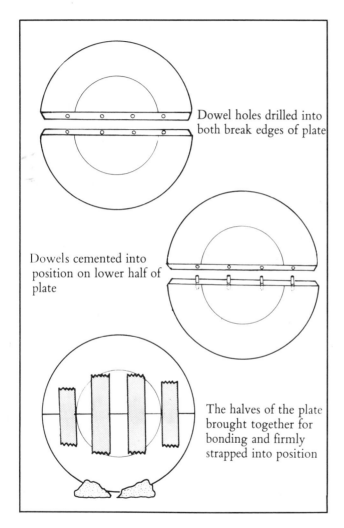

Dowel holes drilled into both break edges of plate

Dowels cemented into position on lower half of plate

The halves of the plate brought together for bonding and firmly strapped into position

right through the hole and out on the other side. When the filling is almost dry smooth it down with your finger or a rag dipped in meths, making sure that your finger or the rag is not too wet. Always be sure that the rivet hole is quite clean, and free of stains and old cement before filling.

Dowelling

When a broken object is large and heavy and the join is likely to be subjected to some strain, dowelling is recommended. This means that you reinforce the join in the piece by supporting it with internal pins of stainless steel or brass, as well as bonding with adhesive. In order to do this, holes must be drilled in the ceramic with an electric drill and diamond-pointed drill head.

The use of the drill There are several drills from which to choose and quite good results can be achieved with a small battery-driven hand drill. However, an electric drill with a flexible shaft is most usually recommended. The drill points required for drilling porcelain must be diamond tipped. These are expensive but with careful use will have a good working life.

When drilling on porcelain with a diamond tip, it is important to keep the tip cool, or both the tip and the motor will burn out. One method is to

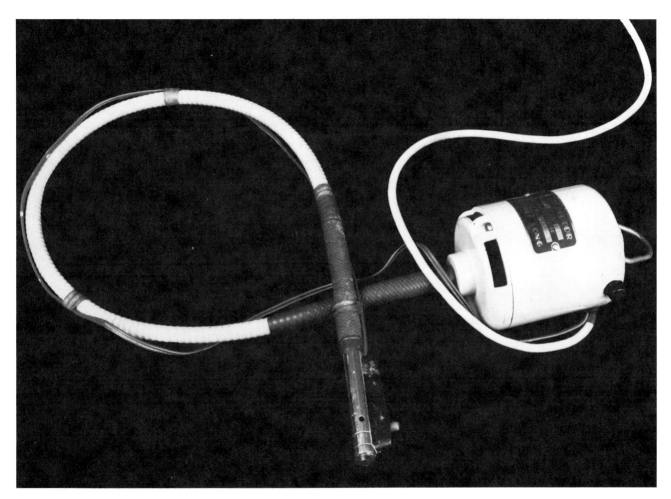

Electric drill with flexible shaft

work under a dripping tap so that the area being drilled and the diamond point have a continual drip of cold water on them. I do not recommend working with the ceramic and drill point completely under water, as working with water and electricity can be extremely dangerous, and when the ceramic is totally immersed the danger is greatly increased. Another method is to have an assistant standing by, dripping water over the drill point and the drilling area as you work.

Do not let your drill run for long periods and get too hot.

Always wear some sort of protective covering over the eyes as dust particles tend to fly around at high speed and could cause considerable damage if they fly into the eyes.

Method of dowelling

1. Cut dowels of stainless steel or brass to the required length.
2. On the broken edge of one side of the ceramic, place a small dot of paint where each hole is to be made. (The number of holes necessary depends on the size and type of the object to be reinforced. In a large heavy plate or bowl, two holes in the thick part of the base and one about 12 mm ($\frac{1}{2}$ in) from the rim at either end are sufficient.)
3. While the paint is still wet bring the two sides together; in this way both sides will be marked accurately where the holes have to be drilled.
4. Drill the holes, using a fine diamond point. The size of the hole should be slightly bigger than the dowel so as to take the dowel and cementing composition. Do not, however, make the holes too deep but just large enough for the dowels to fit about half way into the hole.
5. When all the holes are drilled, and before you apply the adhesive, fit the pieces together and check that the holes on the two sides match in perfect alignment and the dowels are all the same size.
6. Mix up some Araldite (2-tube or AY103/HY956 – *Devcon Clear, Epotek 301 and hardener or RP103 and H956*) and, putting aside a small quantity for bonding the edges of the piece, with the remainder mix up a good strong composition with the addition of plaster of Paris or kaolin.
7. Fill the holes with composition.
8. Fit the dowels firmly into position in the holes. It is sometimes recommended to let the dowels set hard in the composition in the holes before joining the two sides together.
9. Prepare the other section of the piece to receive the dowelled half. It should either be supported firmly in a sandbox or clamped securely.
10. Fill the holes in this half of the piece with composition, but not too much so that it does not

Plate showing dowels in position on break edge

ooze out over the sides of the holes on to the break edge when the dowels sink into them.

11. Smear this break edge with the Araldite which was put aside for bonding.

12. Strap the two halves together very firmly and leave to dry, well supported in a sandbox or suitable support.

The same method of dowelling is used in fitting broken handles to cups, jugs, etc., and for fitting broken limbs back on to figurines.

43

Rubbing

Great care must be taken in rubbing down the dry composition with abrasive papers. It is a most important part in the work of restoring ceramics, and possibly takes up more than half of the time used to restore a piece of china. Scratching the surrounding glaze and damaging the decoration must be avoided. Also watch carefully, in your enthusiasm to rub down the fillings, that you do not rub too much away and so have the tedious business of mixing up more composition and refilling.

Cut the abrasive paper (wet and dry, or Flex-I-Grit) into small squares about 4 cm square ($1\frac{1}{2}$ sq in). These can be folded again to make smaller squares or rolled to make small cylinder-like paper files. The rubbing down movement should be worked in a circular direction starting from the centre and working outwards – try not to rub across the glaze and undamaged area.

Start with a fairly coarse paper proceeding to finer grade papers. For example, start with wet and dry 600 and finish with wet and dry 1000 or 1200 or a fine Flex-I-Grit paper, 400 to 600.

When using wet and dry abrasive keep dipping the paper in clean water when rubbing over the repaired area and wipe the area frequently with a wet cloth as sludge soon builds up.

The object is to rub the composition down so that it is smooth and flush with the unbroken area and when you lightly rub your finger along the surface you can feel only the smooth surface with no ridges or rough edges.

When all the fillings have been completed and rubbed down so that they are smooth and free of all holes and imperfections, and you can only be sure of this by closely scrutinizing the repair through a magnifying glass, polish the piece by putting a little Solvol Autosol cream on a clean cloth and rubbing it gently over the whole surface. Then buff it to a good clean finish ready for painting.

Large areas can be ground down with the electric drill with silicon grinding points and special carborundum wheels. Do not use diamond drill heads on composition. Great care must be taken when using the drill for grinding down composition that it does not travel off the repair area on to the undamaged surface and destroy the glaze on the surrounding area.

Remember to have clean hands during all the operations, constantly washing your hands and dusting them with French chalk. You will be handling the fillings a good deal and dirty hands will produce a very grubby looking work.

5. SIMPLE MODELLING

Tools, equipment and materials necessary

Tools
Boxwood modelling tools
Various probes, old dental hand
    tools
Wire cutters
Stainless steel scissors, 10 cm
    (4 in)
Palette knife
Scalpel handles and blades;
    Swann-Morton handles nos.
    3 and 4, blades nos. 10, 11,
    15, 23
Dividers
Callipers
Electric drill with diamond drill
    head and discs
Needle files
Riffler files
Magnifying glass

Materials
Araldite epoxy resin, 2-tube

pack (*Devcon Clear*)
Araldite AY103 with hardener
    HY956 (*Epotek 301 and
    hardener or RP103 and hardener
    H956*)
Filler powders: Dental plaster,
    fine-grade or plaster of Paris
    (*Hydrocal*)
Kaolin
Polyfilla, interior
Polyfilla, fine-surface, ready-
    mixed (*Polyfix*)
Sylmasta 2-pack (*Elmer's epoxy
    resin*)
Titanium dioxide
Methylated spirit (*Denatured
    ethyl alcohol*)
Household bleach
French chalk or talc
White spirit (*Mineral spirit,
    Stodard solvent*)
White modelling putty,

Plasticine (*Plastelina Roma
    Italian No. 2 white*)
Brass dowelling wire 16, 18, 19
    gauge
Stainless steel rods
Abrasive papers, wet and dry
    320–1000/1200; Flex-I-Grit
    400/600
Carborundum discs and burrs

General equipment
Mixing tiles and saucers
Clean cloths and rags
White absorbent kitchen paper
Plastic and glass containers
Graded medicine glass
Transparent adhesive tape,
    Sellotape (*Scotchtape*)
Tape dispenser
Wooden cocktail sticks
Sandbox containing silver sand
    61 × 36 × 16 cm (24 × 14 × 6 in)

In the course of restoration work you will inevitably, sooner or later, have to replace a missing limb, an arm, a leg, a foot or hand or a wing or perhaps some small object held in the hand such as a basket, fishing rod, gun or some musical instrument from a figurine. If there is no indication as to what the missing embellishment may be, or in just what position it was in, it is always advisable to research very thoroughly before attempting to replace the missing piece. Visit museums and libraries and search through books on porcelain and you will usually find either a similar piece or a photograph of it. You should not resort to your own imagination until every possible channel has been followed in attempting to find the identity of the missing piece.

Modelling missing embellishments can be one of the most satisfying aspects of mending broken china, and it is here that a knowledge of sculpture can be most helpful. Your artistic ability, too, can come into play, but it is most important that your work should be in keeping with the original style of the piece.

Compositions used in modelling

The compositions used in modelling are the same as those used in filling cracks. You can use 2-tube Araldite (*Devcon Clear*) or AY103/HY956 (*Epotek 301 and hardener or RP103 and H956*) with a small amount of titanium dioxide, kaolin or plaster of Paris mixed to a good stiff paste, about the consistency of pastry.

Sylmasta (*Elmer's Epoxy Resin*) is also an excellent putty for modelling, but a small amount of Araldite should be added to improve the adhesive quality.

Polyfilla mixed with water is also used very successfully for modelling up pieces of pottery. The powder and water should be mixed to the consistency of a good thick stiff paste.

The choice of composition for modelling pieces will ultimately rest with the restorer who will also have to decide whether to model the missing part directly on to the broken piece or to model it away from the piece, and when complete attach it to the broken area. This again will depend on the restorer's deftness and the nature of the break and the pieces to be restored. No hard and fast rules can be laid down, although in restoring limbs direct modelling, i.e. modelling the missing piece directly on to the broken area, with the use of dowels, can be the more satisfactory method. Embellishments, on the other hand, are often easier to model indirectly, i.e. away from the piece, to be attached to the piece when they are completed.

Replacing the missing limbs on a figurine is a

painstaking and not always very simple operation. If there is only one arm missing, the remaining arm will be a good guide from which to work, regarding the size and length. With callipers take measurements of the arm: the length from the shoulder to the elbow, and the elbow to the wrist, the thickness of the arm, the wrist, the hand and fingers. Study the good arm very closely, noting the position of the hands, the slope of the arm, etc. Take time; handle the piece, until you feel that you have really got to know it well. Do not be put off if you have had no experience in sculpting. I have seen a most excellent piece of modelling done by someone with no experience whatsoever in the art of sculpting. It is a matter of having the courage to 'have a go' and then plenty of practice and patience.

Let us assume it is more convenient to model the arm directly on to the figure. First place the figure in a sandbox or firmly fixed into a support of modelling putty in the most convenient position for working. A blob of Araldite is then applied to the broken area and allowed to set to a thick and rubbery consistency. A piece of wire or a pin, cut roughly to size and then notched or roughened with a file so that it gives the composition a good base on which to adhere, is bent to shape, pushed into the Araldite, and supported until set. Cut the wire or pin to the same length as the arm, measured from the point of the break to the centre of the palm. In larger, heavier pieces a hole may have to be drilled into the china and the wire dowel inserted into the hole as described in the section on dowelling, page 40. Again, the wire or pin must be bent at the elbow in accordance with the piece being copied or a photograph of the piece being copied. The point of the wrist joint should be marked.

When the Araldite has dried and the wire is firmly anchored, you can start applying thin layers of your chosen composition, wrapping it around the wire and squeezing and pressing it on to the wire with fingers or a tool slightly dampened with water or meths (*denatured ethyl alcohol*). Leave each layer to dry and harden before applying the next layer. Start to shape on the second layer, narrowing down at the wrist and leaving a slightly thicker area on the upper inside arm for the muscle. Constantly check your measurements on the good arm with your callipers. Remember that the wire ends in the centre of the palm of the hand so do not take the composition up to the end of the wire, but only up to where the wire is marked at the wrist, as you will be building up the hand on this bare end of the wire.

When modelling an arm points to remember are:

1. If the arm is covered with a sleeve, note carefully

the fall of the folds of the cloth on the good arm if there is one from which to copy. Make deep indentations with a wet modelling tool, following the lines and creases of the folds.

2. In cases where both limbs are missing from the original piece you will have to depend on a similar piece to guide you in attaining the correct size and proportions. If you are having to depend on a photograph or sketch, a similar piece not being available, extra care will be needed in checking measurements and getting the proportions right.

Freehand modelling is a painstaking process but ultimately extremely satisfying. Do not despair if your first attempts are not all you would wish. This kind of work requires much practice and with it will come the improvements for which you are aiming.

When there is an identical piece to copy the work is very much simplified as a mould can then be taken and a cast made of the model. This will be dealt with in chapter 6 on moulds and casts.

Modelling hands can be a fiddly job, especially if the hand is very small. The hand can be modelled up in one piece but it is usually more successful to model a hand in sections, from the wrist to the knuckles, the thumb and finally the fingers. Each finger is rolled out and fitted separately over a thin piece of wire or pin which has been embedded in the modelled-up hand at the knuckles.

When the arm has dried thoroughly and has been smoothed into shape, push a thin layer of composition on to the wire protruding from the modelled-up arm at the wrist. Now start to shape the hand from the wrist to the knuckles, always checking measurements with your callipers. While the putty is still soft push the wire or pins for the fingers in place. For small hands and fingers electrical fuse wire can be used. Fine dowelling wire can be used to reinforce fingers on larger pieces. The wires should be shorter than the overall length of the fingers so that the fingers will not end up too long when the pins have been covered with composition.

Roll out a thin piece of composition, fit on to the wires with a dampened modelling tool or cocktail stick, and shape to correct form. When you are satisfied that the hand is the right size and in the right position leave to dry. It should be noted that the finished arm and hand should be just fractionally smaller than the original as you will have to take into account the layers of paint and glaze which are to follow.

It is sometimes possible to attach fingers to the hands without the use of pins and wires, by rolling out a piece of composition like a long very thin sausage. When it is almost set but still flexible, the fingers are cut to size, shaped and left to set. Each finger is then attached to the hand by means of a tiny blob of adhesive, and when dry another layer of composition can be gently applied to each finger to bring them up to the correct size and shape. Alternatively, fingers can be built up on the hand by degrees. A small drop of pure Araldite adhesive is applied to the point on which the finger is to be rebuilt. It helps to roughen this area before applying the adhesive to prevent it slipping off, as minute quantities will be used if the fingers to be replaced are very small. Allow the adhesive to get a little tacky (about 10 to 15 minutes) then apply a small amount of composition mixture rolled to approximately the diameter of the finger. Allow to dry, then add a small amount of composition about the same size as on the first application. This will usually adhere without the help of a fine smear of adhesive. By repeating this process the finger can gradually be built up by degrees. It is a very slow process and care is necessary in the smoothing and shaping as you proceed in order to prevent a lot of rubbing down later.

In modelling hands, points to remember are:

1. Hands are usually in a relaxed attitude with the fingers slightly bent.
2. The base of the thumb starts in the centre of the palm and not at the side of the hand.
3. Always take very careful measurements, checking constantly with your callipers.

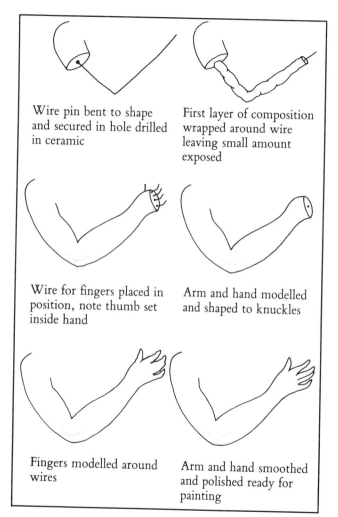

Wire pin bent to shape and secured in hole drilled in ceramic

First layer of composition wrapped around wire leaving small amount exposed

Wire for fingers placed in position, note thumb set inside hand

Arm and hand modelled and shaped to knuckles

Fingers modelled around wires

Arm and hand smoothed and polished ready for painting

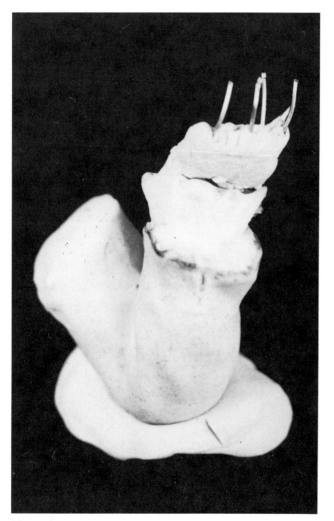

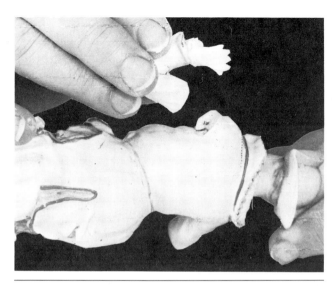

Far left: Broken arm supported in putty with hand modelled in composition and wire pins placed in position for fingers

Left: Fingers and hand modelled and ready for smoothing down

Above: With the figure supported on its side a hole is drilled and a dowel inserted. A corresponding hole is drilled in the arm in correct alignment and it is then bonded to the figure. As it is difficult to strap the arm in position, putty will be used to wedge it in position.

Right: The restored figurine

When the modelled arm and hand are completely dry, they must be rubbed down and given a smooth unblemished surface. A small piece of abrasive paper folded to size and carefully drawn down between the fingers and fine needle files used with care will smooth the putty very satisfactorily. Ensure that the new arm is satin smooth and free of blemishes especially where it joins the broken edge.

Modelling a missing cup handle

If you do not have an identical undamaged cup from which to take a cast for replacing a missing handle, you will have to make one. Here, again, before you attempt to replace the handle, search through books on porcelain, visit museums and exhibitions. It is surprising how many different shapes and designs there are in cup and jug handles and a handle that is over-large or too small or in the wrong style or shape for the period will be only too obvious when the work is complete. When you are satisfied that your choice of shape of handle is appropriate, plan how you are going to support the cup when you are working on it. Building up a cup handle is a long job and you will need to wedge the cup firmly in place. Rest it in a sandbox or wedge it between two large pads of modelling putty, balanced at the right angle for easy working.

Having chosen the shape of your handle, sketch it out on a piece of stiff paper or cardboard in the appropriate size for the object. Now take a piece of brass wire, no thicker than $\frac{1}{3}$ of the diameter of the handle you are to model, and cut it a fraction longer than the finished handle. Notch the wire with a file at random intervals, so that the composition will adhere to the wire with greater ease. Place the wire over your sketch down the centre of the handle bending it to the required shape.

Mark the centre of the stubs where the handle has broken off.

Snip the wire to fit on to the stubs in the correct position.

Mix up some Araldite and put a small blob on to each stub; leave the Araldite until it is rubbery and tacky, then put a small blob on each end of the wire.

Build up a column of modelling putty from the side of the cup to act as a support for the wire skeleton handle. Place the wire into position, and push each end into the now rubbery adhesive on each stub coinciding with the centre marks. Make sure that the modelling putty holds the wire firmly while the adhesive sets.

If the Araldite has run down on to the cup, lift it up with a stick and wrap it round the base of the wire handle. Do not worry about the rough finish

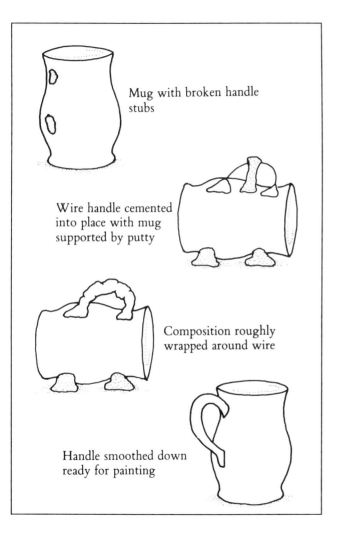

Mug with broken handle stubs

Wire handle cemented into place with mug supported by putty

Composition roughly wrapped around wire

Handle smoothed down ready for painting

of the adhesive as this will act as a good key for the composition when the modelling commences.

Check that the wire is in its correct position and the ends of the wire are in the right place. Put aside to dry.

When the adhesive has set remove the putty column. Check that the adhesive has dried firmly around the base of the wire by lifting the cup by the wire handle. If it feels loose, you will have to start again. If it is firm you can proceed to the next stage.

Clean adhesive away if it has spread beyond the broken area of the stubs on to the cup.

Mix up a good stiff composition and roll out a thin sausage about the length of the handle. You will be putting on more than two layers of composition before the handle is complete so keep the first roll of composition very thin.

Damp the wire and pinch on the thin roll of composition with dampened fingers. It is not necessary to shape too carefully at this stage. Set aside to dry.

Add successive thin layers, working them well down to the ends of the wire. If the stub is raised do not let the composition stop at the top of the stub but allow it to spread down a little over the stub.

Gradually build up the handle with successive layers of composition. For the final layer, wet the

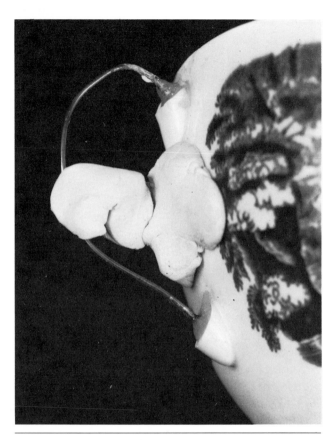

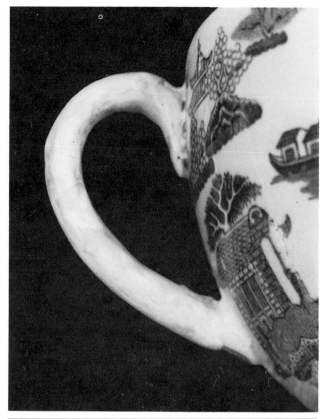

Notched wire has been fixed into position on the handle stubs with blobs of Araldite. The column of putty holds it in position

Cup handle after final layer of composition has been modelled on to the wire

Completed handle

previous layer with moistened fingers, lay the final composition roll along the handle, and pinch it into position with damp fingers. Make sure the composition flows a little over the stubs.

Allow to dry. If there are any little holes or blemishes fill in and adjust with a little additional composition and smooth over with damp fingers. Allow to dry completely.

Smooth down with abrasive paper in preparation for painting.

Teapot spouts

One of the most vulnerable parts of a piece of china is the end of the spout of a teapot. Once more I do recommend that you check in books on porcelain or in museums for the exact shape of the spout, if you have no similar piece to guide you.

A teapot will usually need a good deal of cleaning as there is sure to be much tannin staining. Household bleach usually removes this stain with ease.

Apply a thin smear of Araldite to the broken edges, then mix up a good stiff and very dry composition. Place a thin roll of composition along the broken edge, squeezing it back over and under the edge. Then, with your fingers dampened, but not wet, with water or meths, ease the composition forward to form the lip of the spout. Squeeze and press it out to the correct shape. The addition of a small amount of composition may be necessary if you have made the lip too thin or too small. If you have made the lip too big and too long, support the composition with your finger and cut the excess putty to a more suitable length with a pair of scissors, the blades of which have been dipped into meths or French chalk.

When the lip is just a fraction longer than the correct length, support it with adhesive tape or a roll of modelling putty and leave to dry. Shape with needle files and smooth down with fine abrasive paper rolled into a cylindrical shape.

Flowers and leaves

You will always have some composition left over after you have made up a quantity to do your fillings and modelling and you will be loath to throw it away.

It is not necessary to waste this left-over composition. It can be rolled into different lengths and sizes in a sausage-like roll and cut to make dowels. If you leave the composition for half an hour or so it will not be so pliable and will be less ready to curl back upon itself.

This left-over composition can be very useful in making petals for flowers or leaves. A collection of these kept in a jar are useful when you find you

have to replace a missing leaf or petal on a piece of ceramic.

1. Dust a tile or clean piece of paper with French chalk or kaolin.
2. Roll out the composition into a smooth flat piece approximately 3 mm ($\frac{1}{8}$ in) thick and cut the shape required with a sharp blade dipped in meths. Veins on the leaves and markings on petals can be made with a cocktail stick or modelling tool.

Leaves and petals are usually curved. The best way to get the necessary curve in the leaf or petal is to bend them over a collar of modelling composition. This collar is made by rolling out a sausage-like roll of composition and joining the ends so that it looks like a ring doughnut.

Another simple way to make petals and leaves is to dust the palm of your hand with French chalk, take a small piece of composition and press it into the palm of the hand, then lift it with a cocktail stick, rolling it slightly over at one end to give it more shape, and drape it over the doughnut-shaped collar of composition. Several little petals can be made this way. Allow to set hard and then attach in position on the ceramic with Araldite.

In many cases, half-petals will be missing. These can be built up directly on to the remaining half of the petal and supported with a little pad of modelling composition while setting.

Flowers and leaves modelled from left-over composition.
Some of the petals are drying over a ring of putty

The use of the drill

The drill is used a lot in modelling, for shaping and grinding down. Please see the detailed instructions on using the drill on page 40, and particularly bear in mind the safety precautions you should take.

Diamond Hi-Di 63 drill discs are good for making grooves in china, but never use the discs in composition as they will clog and be useless in a very short time.

Steel burrs can be used for fine shaping of composition, shaping limbs and hands and getting into awkward corners. Steel burrs should not be used on porcelain. Clean the burrs with a soft wire brush. Rubbing with a little talc or French chalk before use helps to prevent clogging.

The drill can be used for grinding down large areas of composition filling, but great attention must be paid to ensure that the surrounding surface glaze is not damaged. A selection of miniature carborundum grinding wheels will be necessary for grinding down composition. Grinding with a drill should be done carefully and slowly. Do not press hard, but rather let the wheel move with only a slight guiding touch. Hold the handle of the flexible drive firmly, so as not to let the wheel run away on to the glaze and damage it.

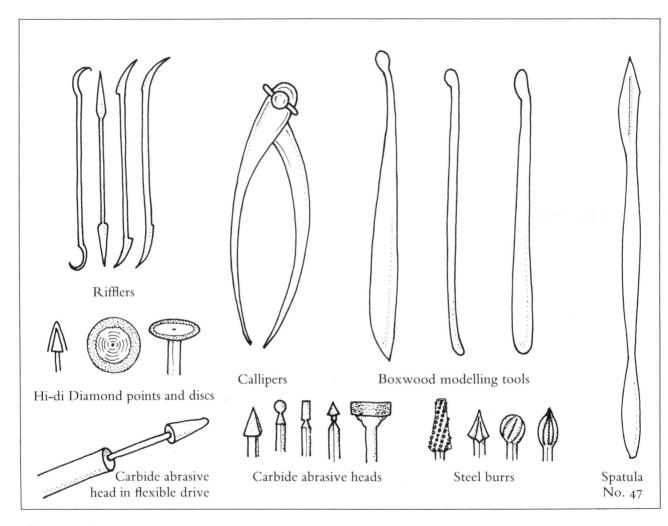

Rifflers

Hi-di Diamond points and discs

Carbide abrasive
head in flexible drive

Callipers

Carbide abrasive heads

Boxwood modelling tools

Steel burrs

Spatula
No. 47

6. MOULDS AND CASTS

Tools, equipment and materials necessary

Tools
Needle files

Materials
Araldite epoxy resin, 2-tube pack (*Devcon Clear*)
Araldite AY103 with hardener HY956 (*Epotek 301 and hardener or RP103 and hardener H956*)
Filler powders: Dental plaster, fine-grade or plaster of Paris (*Hydrocal*)
Kaolin
Mercaptan impression material

Titanium dioxide
Rubber latex, Qualitex PV or Revultex (*Kwikmold or Pliatex*)
Vinamold Red
White modelling putty, Plasticine (*Plastelina Roma Italian No. 2 white*)
Woodflour or paper dust
Wax releasing agent, slip wax (Butcher's wax)
Solvol Autosol polish
Abrasive papers, wet and dry 320–1000/1200; Flex-I-Grit 400/600

French chalk or talc
Vaseline

General equipment
Wooden cocktail sticks
Various plastic and glass containers
Cotton wool
Small mixing bowls
Mixing tiles
Graded medicine glass
Saucepan with lid
Transparent adhesive tape, Sellotape (Scotchtape)
Tape dispenser

While freehand modelling can be enjoyable and the results highly satisfying, it is often a very slow process, though there is, of course, no other method when you have only a sketch or photograph from which to copy the object to be modelled. If, however, you are fortunate enough to find an undamaged piece identical to the one requiring restoration, your work will not only be hastened but also greatly simplified. You will be able to take a mould from the undamaged piece, then pour or press the casting material into this mould and an identical piece will be produced.

Of all the moulding materials, rubber latex is the most versatile and widely used, for thickness can be varied by the number of coats applied in accordance with the size of the model from which the mould is taken. Latex can be removed with ease from the model, and for this reason this type of mould is called a flexible mould. It is extremely useful when there is some undercut on the model. That is when the decoration or embellishments on the ceramic is so built up that it makes it difficult to remove the mould from the original.

The object from which the mould is to be taken should be thoroughly cleaned and inspected for any imperfections as these will ultimately appear in the reproduction. It is therefore as well to be prepared for them and if necessary effect a few minor repairs to the model before commencing with the mould. Do not use rubber latex moulds on metals, marbles and ivories.

When making a rubber latex mould the following steps should be taken:

1. Pour some latex into a small container (always keep latex well covered as it will congeal and discolour if left open to the air).
2. Dip a cocktail stick on to which some cotton wool is rolled at one end (or a cotton wool 'bud' obtained in packs from any chemist), into latex

Rubber latex being applied to the head of the figure to make a mould. No wood flour will be used to stiffen the mould due to the under cut.

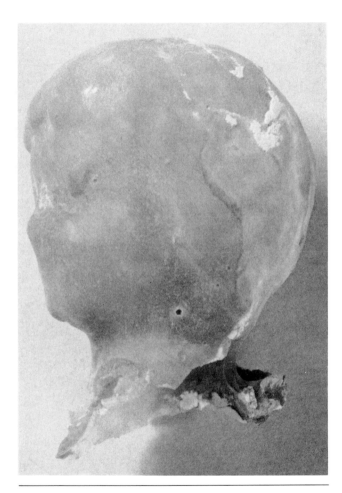

Completed mould removed from head

and apply smoothly on to the model in a thin layer. Work evenly and slowly in order to avoid creating air bubbles. The first layer is an important one; it must be quite smooth. Any imperfections in this layer will spoil the cast. If any air bubbles should appear, prick them out with a pin. Leave to dry for 8 to 12 hours. The latex turns brown when it dries.

3. Repeat second, third and subsequent layers in the same way, leaving several hours for each layer to dry before applying the next layer. If the mould has a slightly milky white patch anywhere in it, it is not dry, and must be left until it has the brown appearance of the dried latex all over. Five to seven layers produce a strong, but easily removed mould.

4. Before peeling the completed mould from the model dust it with talc or French chalk to prevent the dry latex sticking to itself.

When replacing large missing areas from ceramics you will need a more rigid mould as a good strong support for the composition.

Apply the first layer as described above, followed by a few more layers, always making sure that each layer is thoroughly dry before applying the next layer. For the final layer, pour some rubber latex into a container, into this mix some wood flour (fine sifted sawdust, obtainable from any builder's merchant) or paper dust to a thick creamy consistency, and apply to the mould with a palette knife. Leave to dry. The length of drying time depends on the thickness of the layer, which should be between 3 mm and 6 mm ($\frac{1}{8}$ in and $\frac{1}{4}$ in), depending on the size of the repair, but it can take up to 12 hours to dry. Do not apply more than two layers of the thickened latex.

Where a very large and extremely rigid support mould is required, for example for a large curved area on the side of a bowl, or a plate with most of one side missing, the mould must still be flexible enough to be removed from the model in safety. To achieve this more rigid type of mould, the back of the latex mould can be coated with a plaster of Paris (*hydrocal*) cast. The latex mould must be quite dry before the plaster of Paris is applied. It will be necessary to coat the rubber latex with a releasing agent such as Vaseline or a slipwax release agent before applying the plaster of Paris 'mother' so that it can be removed when set and the mould lifted away from the model area. The plaster of Paris is mixed with water to a thick creamy consistency (always add the powder to the water, and when it peaks up above the level of the water this usually means that sufficient powder has been added). This creamy paste is then applied to the latex mould to a depth of about 12 mm ($\frac{1}{2}$ in) and left to dry thoroughly. It will break very easily if an attempt is made to remove it before it is dry. When it is

quite dry it will lift away quite easily from the mould. The mould is then peeled away from the model area and, with its support, is then fitted to the area to be repaired, strapped firmly into position with adhesive tape. Smear a little adhesive on to the broken edges, dust the inside of the mould with talc or French chalk, then fill with composition mixture. Always make sure that the mould extends beyond the broken area.

For very small moulds, such as flowers and small hands, where it would be difficult to peel off a stiff mould, only a few coats of latex are necessary and no stiffening agent should be added.

Casting materials

Araldite AY103/HY956 (*Epotek 301 and hardener or RP103 and H956*)
For detailed information on this resin and hardener, see page 36. When mixed with plaster of Paris, titanium dioxide or kaolin it becomes a very useful, easy flowing casting material.

Mix in the proportion of 5 parts AY103 to 1 part HY956. When only a small amount is required, use a small kitchen measuring spoon for measuring out the quantities on to a clean mixing saucer. Always wipe the spoon clean of AY103 before putting it into the hardener HY956. If a larger quantity is

Rubber latex mould on head of Chinese figure. Note the putty collar to prevent latex dripping down. The cast taken from the mould is shown at right

required pour five parts AY103 into a graded measuring glass, add one part HY956 and stir thoroughly together. Leave a little of the mixture, covered, on a tile, well blended with some titanium dioxide. Leave the remaining mixture in the measuring glass for 20 minutes. Keep the glass covered. After 20 minutes add the Araldite and titanium mixture to the mixture in the glass and stir well. This prevents the AY103/HY956 from yellowing. The casting composition must be fluid enough to be poured easily into a mould so do not leave it standing for too long as it will get tacky and difficult to pour. A small amount of plaster of Paris or kaolin can be added to the Araldite mixture to give the cast more body before filling the mould, but care must be taken not to make it too thick and so reduce the pouring consistency.

Always dust the inside of the mould with talc powder or French chalk. When filling small moulds, dip a spatula or metal stick into the liquid Araldite and let it drip down in a small steady trickle along the side of the mould so that the air can be pushed out and not become trapped.

When using a two-part mould the casting composition need not be so fluid. The mixture may stand a little longer (30 to 40 minutes) so that it becomes easy to handle when mixed with titanium dioxide and plaster of Paris or kaolin to a fairly good stiff composition.

Two-tube Araldite mixed up to a fairly good stiff composition as described in the chapter on modelling can also be effectively used as a casting material in a two-part mould.

Fine white plaster of Paris or dental plaster
(*hydrocal*)

Mix the powder with water to a pouring consistency. Always add the powder to the water till it forms peaks above the level of the water. Pour the mixture very carefully and very slowly into the mould, tapping the container from time to time to avoid air bubbles. When this type of cast has been removed from the mould it should be coated with an Araldite mixture and warmed to draw the Araldite into the material to give it added strength.

Examples of the use of rubber latex moulds

As a support mould in replacing a missing piece from a plate or saucer

When a large area is missing from a plate or saucer, bowl or cup, etc., it cannot be successfully built up with composition without the help of a good rigid support, and in this case a rubber latex mould is used.

Having first cleaned the object with acetone, examine it very carefully and note if there is a raised pattern or embellishment, for you will have to decide on which side it will be more practical for you to take the mould. In the case of raised patterns, the mould must be taken from the patterned side if at all possible.

Measure the size of the missing area and mark out a larger area on the undamaged side of the plate. Build up a wall of modelling putty around the area to prevent the latex dripping down.

Pour some rubber latex into a container. Dip a wooden cocktail stick around one end of which is wrapped some cotton wool (or a cotton wool bud) into the latex and apply to the undamaged area, taking it up and over the rim and extending well on to the measured out markings. Make sure that there are no air holes in the latex and that this first coat is quite smooth and free of imperfections. Any little air bubbles can be pricked out with a pin or sharp pointed instrument. Leave to dry thoroughly before applying the next coat. Apply several coats, depending on the size of the missing area; you will want a very firm mould if the area to fill is a large one. Allow 8 to 12 hours for each coat of latex to dry. Finally mix together some wood flour or paper dust and latex in a container to the consistency of a thin paste and apply with a knife or spatula about 6 mm ($\frac{1}{4}$ in) in depth. If the area is large and curved you may find it necessary to have a more rigid support to prevent the mould from sagging. Allow the mould to dry, then apply some vaseline or slipwax release agent (*butcher's wax*) to the mould. Mix up a creamy paste of plaster of Paris and apply to about 12 mm ($\frac{1}{2}$ in) in depth and leave to dry.

When quite dry, carefully prise the plaster of Paris 'mother' away from the latex mould. Lift the latex mould away from the plate. Strap the mould, with its plaster of Paris support, firmly over the missing area making sure that the mould fits well and is securely in place. Dust the mould with a little French chalk.

Mix up some AY103/HY956 and a little titanium dioxide and apply a thin coat to the broken edge. Also apply a thin coat of Araldite to the mould. Make sure that all the mould surface is covered and the Araldite coating is free of air bubbles. Now add kaolin or plaster of Paris to your Araldite mixture, and mix until it is stiff but pliable. Press it into the mould a little at a time. Do not put it all in in one go, but work with a small amount at a time, pressing it well down and smoothing it over, using a spatula or a finger dipped in meths to smooth the last layer.

The mould should be removed when the composition has set. There will be some filing down to do and minor imperfections will need to be corrected by the addition of a little more composition and rubbing down and shaping.

A mould to replace the missing part of an openwork plate

Follow the same procedure in making a rigid mould for replacing a missing area on the rim of a plate, cup or bowl. You should pay great attention to pattern and design; the mould must be taken from a part of the plate which corresponds exactly in design to that of the missing area. The mould must also be taken on the side where there is the most detail.

Roll out a piece of modelling putty and place it under the rim of the plate on the reverse side to the one on which the mould is to be taken. This is to prevent latex from going too far through the holes. Start with a thin coat of latex, making sure it is smooth and free of air bubbles. Allow to dry. Follow with a few more coats, depending on the size of the holes in the openwork design of the plate. Follow up with a final coat of latex mixed with a little wood flour or paper dust to the consistency of thin paste. It is important to check that the holes have been filled correctly. Leave to dry thoroughly. Remove the mould and strap firmly into place with adhesive tape making sure the lattice work and the design match with those along the broken edge. Be sure the mould is tightly strapped. Dust mould with French chalk. Mix up AY103/HY956 with some titanium dioxide and spread a small amount on the break edges and over

Plate with piece missing from fretted edge

the surface of the mould. Mix the rest of the Araldite as before with kaolin or plaster of Paris into a thick pliable paste; press this into the mould and allow to dry. Remove the mould. Any inaccuracies will have to be rubbed down or improved

66

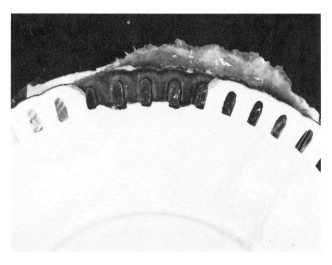

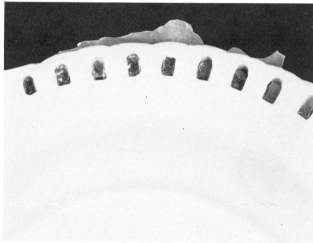

Top left: Plate with rubber latex mould which has been taken from further round the plate. The plaster of Paris 'mother' holds the mould in position for filling with composition

Bottom left: Plate with filling packed into mould

Above: The composition set and mould removed ready for some trimming and rubbing down

Overleaf: The restored plate

In taking a mould from a cup handle the following steps should be taken:

1. Clean object from which mould is to be taken.
2. Make a pattern of the inside of the handle in greaseproof paper. Cut out the pattern.
3. Fill the inside of the handle with modelling putty packed tightly against the ceramic surface.
4. Build a small wall in modelling putty to form a box around the handle in order to stop the latex rolling down and dripping off the cup.
5. Dab latex on one side of the handle with a cocktail stick around one end of which cotton wool has been rolled. Take care there are no air bubbles. Leave to set. The latex is a light brown colour and transparent when it is dry. Apply three or four coats, making sure that each coat is dry before applying the next coat.
6. Carefully remove the modelling putty from the inside of the handle; smear this part of the latex with Vaseline; being careful not to let the Vaseline get on to the ceramic. Put in the paper pattern.
7. Apply latex to the second side of the handle in exactly the same way.
8. Mix the latex with wood flour or paper dust to the consistency of a paste. Apply with a palette

with more composition. Finally, smooth the holes with needle files or abrasive paper in tight rolls, drawn back and forth inside the holes. Smooth down thoroughly and polish with Solvol Autosol ready for painting.

A putty wall is built around the handle and putty is also packed into the area inside the handle. A paper pattern of inside the cup handle is at right

knife or spatula carefully to cover the whole area and leave to dry for approximately 12 hours.

9. Remove the mould. Take out the paper pattern and wipe off all the Vaseline. Smear a small amount of latex over this area (i.e. the inside of the cup handle) and hold together for a few minutes.

10. Make up a small quantity of Araldite AY103/HY956 into which has been mixed a little titanium dioxide. Dip a metal stick or spatula into the liquid Araldite and pour a thin steady stream into one of the open ends, very slowly, letting it run down the side of the mould to push any air out of the other side. Support the mould in a sandbox and leave to set.

11. When quite dry, slit the latex mould where it was sealed at the inside of the handle area with a sharp blade and lift out the Araldite handle ready to fix to the cup. The cast will need rubbing and trimming. It can be fitted to the cup by means of dowels.

Rubber latex being applied to the side of the cup handle

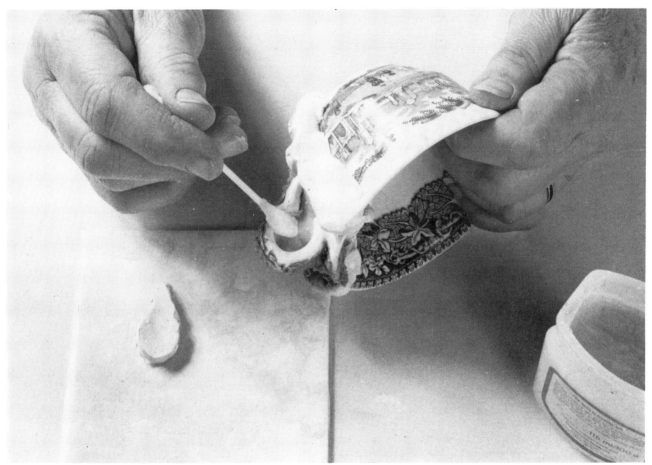

With the putty filling the cup handle removed, the paper pattern is positioned and vaseline is applied before the latex is applied to the second side of the cup.

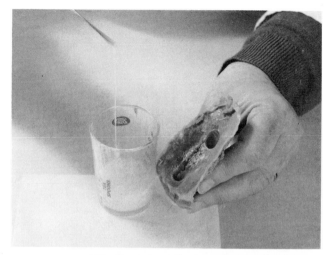

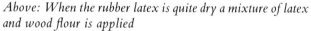

Above: When the rubber latex is quite dry a mixture of latex and wood flour is applied

Top right: Araldite AY103 and HY956 is mixed with some titanium dioxide and dental plaster in a measured glass

Bottom right: When introducing the casting material into the mould allow a fine trickle to run down the side of the mould

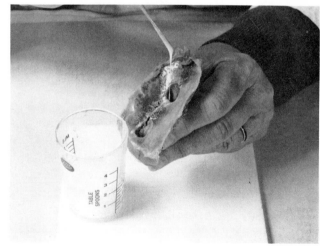

Use of rubber latex as a two-part mould

A two-part mould can be taken from cup handles or handles to bowls and lids, especially when there may be difficulties in making a one-part mould, because of the design and position of the handles.

1. Divide the handle into two equal parts by drawing a line down the centre.
2. Roll out a piece of modelling putty to a thickness of 6 mm ($\frac{1}{4}$ in) and press it firmly into the side of the handle so that it fills the space between the handle and the side of the cup and extends beyond the outer rim of the handle by about 2 cm ($\frac{3}{4}$ in). Press firmly against the side of the cup and check that the handle has sunk sufficiently deeply into the modelling putty, so that the putty comes up to the centre line along the handle. Also making sure that there is no gap between the putty and the ceramic for the latex to drip through.
3. With a cocktail stick or metal tool make holes in the side of the putty which extends beyond the outer rim of the handle. These will form keys for fitting the two halves of the moulds together.
4. Apply a thin coat of latex over the entire area, making sure that the application is smooth and free of air bubbles. Allow to dry. Apply four or five more coats, allowing each coat to dry before applying the next one.

5. Mix up latex and wood flour or paper dust to the consistency of paste and apply this coat fairly thickly. Leave to set for at least 48 hours. When quite dry, remove the modelling putty, making sure all the putty has been removed.
6. Before applying the second half of the mould you will need to apply a releasing agent, so that the two halves do not stick together. Vaseline or slipwax release agent (*butcher's wax*) can be used. Apply this with cotton wool buds over the entire surface of the latex. Be sure that it covers the area fully so that nowhere can the two halves stick together, but avoid putting the releasing agent on the cup handle itself. If you do, wipe it off and clean thoroughly.
7. Apply the second half of the mould exactly as you did the first half. A good smooth first coat is applied to the entire surface followed by 4 or 5 more coats. Each coat must be thoroughly dry before the next coat is applied. Finally apply a good thick coat of rubber latex mixed with wood flour or paper dust. Leave to dry.
8. Remove the two halves when thoroughly dry. They should separate quite easily. Dust with French chalk.
9. Pack casting composition into each mould. Remember when using the two-part mould that the casting composition must be much stiffer and thicker.

At right the handle of the vase has been imbedded in modelling putty. Note the holes for keys. At left the two moulds are shown with completed cast of handle

10. Bring the two halves together, fitting the keys correctly into position. Bind together with rubber bands and leave to set.
11. Pull the two halves apart, carefully remove cast and check for imperfections. It will nearly always be necessary to do some rubbing down, especially along the centre of the handle. Some additional composition may have to be applied to smooth out the shape of the handle.

It will also be necessary to adjust the handle to fit on to the cup with the use of either a hacksaw blade or a file.

In some cases it may be more practicable to fit the handle on with a dowel, drilling a hole in each stub and also in the cast. The handle is then fitted on as described in the chapter on dowelling. The handle is supported by means of a column of modelling putty and adhesive tape while it is drying.

Where a handle is fairly large a plaster of Paris 'mother' can be used to make the mould more rigid.

Hints on making rubber latex moulds

1. When making a mould of a small hand use only three to four coats of latex, without stiffening agent. The AY103/HY956 with titanium dioxide added should be liquid enough to pour into the smallest area. Pour the Araldite down the side of the mould in a fine steady stream. Where there are hands and small fingers at the bottom of the mould, work the casting material well into the fingers and hands, forcing the air out by tapping the mould gently against the work bench to remove air bubbles. Then continue to pour in the Araldite.
2. For all small moulds such as flowers, and where it would be difficult to peel off a stiff mould, only a few coats of latex are necessary and no stiffening should be used.
3. Many coats, at least five or six, can be used for larger moulds of arms and hands.
4. Always peel off from upper arm to wrist.
5. Dust mould with French chalk before removing and always dust mould with French chalk before introducing casting material.
6. Rubber latex can take up to 12 hours to dry depending on room temperature.
7. Make sure each coat is thoroughly dry before applying the next coat.
8. Do not attempt to dry the rubber latex mould by artificial means. It will shrink and peel away.
9. The mould should fit well over the missing area and extend a little beyond it on to the ceramic on either side.

10. Do not use rubber latex on metals, marbles and ivories.

Vinamold Red

Vinamold Red is another very useful material for flexible moulds. Whereas rubber latex moulds take several days to complete, and can only be used for one model, the drying time for Vinamold is a maximum of two hours. It can be reheated and used several times on different models.

Care, however, must be taken in using Vinamold on a porous material. The model should be protected by applying a few thin coats of a resin based lacquer, and allowing it to dry before starting to make the mould.

1. Cut several pieces off the Vinamold block and melt these very slowly in a saucepan kept solely for this purpose. Keep the saucepan covered while the Vinamold is heating. Do not heat the Vinamold too quickly. It should *never* be allowed to boil, as it will turn brown, stick to the sides of the saucepan, go thready and become quite unfit for use. The fumes that come off the heating Vinamold can be most unpleasant, if not harmful, so it is important to work in a well ventilated area and to heat the Vinamold slowly over low heat. Read and follow the instructions that come with the pack most carefully.

2. Warm the model slightly.

3. Build a wall of modelling putty around the model. If there is some undercut, press in modelling putty, packing it carefully into the dents and hollows so that no Vinamold will be trapped, making removal difficult when set.

4. Make sure all joins in the wall are sealed and the putty fits firmly against the ceramic. Smear and press it well down on to the glazed surface to seal it. The size of the box around the model must be large enough to take the liquid rubber, which must completely cover the model without spilling out.

5. Pour the melted Vinamold slowly down the side of the putty wall, tapping the ceramic gently to avoid any air being trapped and so spoiling the mould. Do not make the walls of the mould too thin. Here you must use your own judgement as to the required thickness of the wall, taking into account the ease with which you will be able to pull the mould away from the model. Curing time with Vinamold is approximately one to two hours.

6. When the mould is set and ready to take the casting, dust the inside with French chalk or talc, fill with casting composition and leave to dry. The mould can be cut up and used again.

The use of Vinamold in a two-part mould

When taking a two-part mould, you must decide how you are going to divide the mould. Think about this very carefully, as the correct division can make quite a difference to the ease of making the cast, so plan the sections in advance.

1. Warm the mould.
2. Build up a putty wall around the model, making sure that it is absolutely leak-proof and large enough to hold the liquid Vinamold, without it spilling over the sides.
3. Melt Vinamold as described, and pour it down the side of the putty wall, very slowly, to the halfway level of the model, or wherever you have decided the level of the first half of the mould should be.
4. Allow to dry for about 30 minutes to one hour, then cut out little snips from the side of the mould. These keys will be filled when the second half of the mould is poured on to the first half, and will be a guide to an accurate fit of the two halves.
5. Cut small narrow channels extending about 6 mm ($\frac{1}{4}$ in) out from the model along the rubber. These are made to take excess casting composition when the mould is filled.
6. Melt and pour on the second half of the mould. Take care not to make the walls too thick.
7. Leave to set.
8. When thoroughly set separate the two halves and remove them from the model.
9. Vinamold does not need a releasing agent, but it is advisable to line the inside of the mould with Vaseline or French chalk before introducing the casting agent.
10. Fill with casting composition.
11. Fit the two halves together again, matching the keys. Bind the two halves firmly together with rubber bands and leave to set.

Pressed moulds

In some ceramics the decoration and embellishments are in the form of relief work on the surface of the object and there is no undercut at all. If you wish to reproduce this raised design a pressed mould is used.

Modelling putty

Wet the ceramic so that the mould can be easily removed. Knead the putty well and roll out flat and smooth about 0.317 cm ($\frac{1}{8}$ in) thick. Press the putty firmly on to the design, then carefully pull away from the model. Put the mould in the refrigerator for a few hours to harden. Dust with French chalk, fill with casting material and leave to set.

Mercaptan impression material

This is a quick setting impression compound. It is supplied in two tubes, which must be mixed carefully and thoroughly in equal parts until the colour change is uniform (blue and yellow to green). It sets in about 7 minutes, so a certain amount of speed is necessary when working with this material. It is, however, useful as a pressed mould for simply constructed decorations, ceramics with decorations in relief, and as a support for the sides of plates, cups, bowls, etc., when missing areas are being built up.

Setting times can be marginally adjusted by increasing or decreasing the proportion of catalyst.

All casts should be smoothed down well and completely free of any imperfections. Polish them with Solvol Autosol before painting.

---

7. PAINTING

Tools, equipment and materials necessary

Tools
Sable paint brushes sizes 0–3
  and a flat brush for glazing
Dividers
Palette knife
Magnifying glass

Materials
White spirit (*mineral spirit,
  Stodard solvent*)
Pure turpentine
Acetone
Methylated spirit (*Denatured
  ethyl alcohol*)
Solvol autosol polish
Abrasive papers, wet and dry
  320–1000/1200; Flex–I–Grit
  400/600
Humbrol enamel paints (*Testors
  plastic enamel paints*):
  White, pale blue, black, deep
blue, pale yellow, orange,
deep yellow, dark green,
dark red, light brown, light
red, dark brown.
Humbrol enamel paint thinner
Humbrol clear varnish
Rowneys picture varnish 800
Barbola varnish
Rustins clear gloss varnish
Artists' oil colours in small
  tubes:
  Titanium white, cerulean
  blue, ivory black, burnt
  sienna, Paynes grey,
  cadmium red, ultramarine,
  veridian, burnt umber,
  alizarin crimson, raw umber,
  Naples yellow, raw sienna,
  yellow ochre
Artists' powdered pigments:
  Same colours as oil colours
Cryla colours (*Artists acrylic
  colours*)
Chinaglaze clear lacquer
Chinaglaze Satin
Chinaglaze White
Catalyst (for air-drying)
Thinner/solvent, Phenthin 83
Chintex stoving paints
Chintex thinners
Chintex clear glaze
Chintex glaze thinner/solvent

General equipment
Mixing tiles and saucers
Clean cloths and rags
White absorbent kitchen paper
Fine tracing paper   H pencil
Plastic and glass containers
Small table-top electric cooker

79

The matching of colours for design and painting is the final stage in restoration of china and often the most difficult one. Success here depends first and foremost on the perfection of the work in the early stages, for no amount of painting will ever conceal a poorly bonded, filled or rubbed-down job. Frequently, too, a filling which looks perfect, even through a magnifying glass, or is satin smooth to the touch, will reveal tiny little pin holes and minute imperfections when the first coat of paint is applied. So be prepared for times when you think you are ready to go ahead with painting and finishing only to find you must remove the paint and do a few more corrections in the way of filling in and smoothing over the blemishes. Sometimes only a little more rubbing down will be required but these final touches are well worth the effort. You must have patience and work towards the highest possible standard. It is advisable, therefore, always to brush a thin layer of white paint over the repair, as this will be the best way of finding out if the repair is satin smooth and ready for painting. This coat of white paint can always be quickly removed with white spirit or solvent before it has dried.

Before starting to paint make sure that the piece is thoroughly clean and has been polished with Solvol Autosol.

There are various media that can be used in the repair of china and each restorer will ultimately work in the medium which he finds best for his requirements and the most suitable for the piece on which he is working.

The cold or air-drying method of painting is the simplest and is strongly recommended, as by using this method it is not necessary to apply heat and stove the pieces.

Stoving paint is not recommended for beginners and it cannot be baked in a kitchen cooker as is frequently assumed. However clean this domestic appliance may be, if it is in regular use it will not be sufficiently free of grease for use in china restoration, where scrupulous cleanliness is so important. The smallest amount of grease can seep into a crack and discolour a piece of work. A small table top electric cooker should be obtained solely for this purpose. In addition there can be some quite tragic disasters when delicate porcelain pieces such as Bow China, are heated; they can easily discolour and break when heat is applied.

In all cases the technique of painting is the same, with only slight variations according to the thickness or viscosity of the paints and glazes.

In choosing the painting medium the following points should be observed:
1. The medium should be clear.
2. It should be easy to apply.

3. It should not discolour.
4. It should dry hard so that it can be rubbed down and polished.
5. It should be capable of withstanding reasonable wear and tear (hot water, detergent, etc.).

Humbrol Enamel (*Testors plastic enamel paint*) adequately fills these requirements and it can be obtained in a wide range of colours in small size tins from most model shops. The small tins are best, for if left opened for long periods the enamel tends to harden, and it is more economical to dispose of a small tin than a large one. Humbrol also produce a clear varnish, which can be used as a glaze, but this does have a very distinct yellow tinge which darkens further with time. However Rustins clear gloss varnish can be used with Humbrol enamels as a glaze medium; although this too has a slight yellow tinge it does not appear to darken with age. Rowney's Picture Varnish 800 and Barbola Varnish can all be used effectively with Humbrol Enamels as a glaze medium. White spirit or Humbrol thinner should be used as the solvent with these paints and glazes.

Chinaglaze, previously known as Pheenalite G310, is a good hard clear varnish which, when mixed with a catalyst, can be used as an air-dried glaze. However as the thinner, Phenthin 83, tends to lift the enamel paints, care must be taken that the paint is very dry and the smallest amount of thinner should be mixed into the glaze (a little less than 10% should be used).

Chinaglaze without the catalyst can be stoved at 50°C (120°F) for $1\frac{1}{2}$-2 hours or 66°C (150°F) for 1-$1\frac{1}{2}$ hours but this material is so highly flammable that its use for stoving is not recommended.

Brushes

At least three or four artist's sable brushes should be included in your painting equipment ranging from size 00 to size 3. The brushes should taper to a fine point. You should also have a flat sable brush for applying glaze. It is not a good idea to buy cheap brushes – painting on china is difficult enough for a beginner and you should not impede your progress with inferior tools. A special brush should be kept for gilding.

Special care must be taken to keep brushes clean at all times. Never put a brush away unless it has been cleaned of all paint. Always rinse brushes out in a suitable solvent after use, making sure all paint has been removed, and store them away carefully when they have been thoroughly cleaned and dried.

The most colourful and highly decorated pieces of pottery or porcelain are the easiest to work on, and the most difficult are white or plain coloured pieces. The white tones of pottery or porcelain vary enormously and it will always be necessary to mix the white with greys, blues, browns or yellows to bring it to the matching tone. It is also almost impossible to disguise a join in any plain white or plain coloured porcelain, by painting. In this case the best course to follow is to make a very good join so that there is only a hairline crack showing. It is not necessary to aim to make your repair completely invisible, as this may entail too much painting beyond the repair area. It is far better to have a good neat repair, which is not entirely invisible, than a very over-painted one which will inevitably, in time, produce a large unsightly discoloured area extending far beyond the restoration.

It is one thing to put colours on a canvas, mixing up your own tones and shades, and quite another matter to mix up colours to match shades and tones used on various pieces of porcelain and pottery. Getting it right will depend on your eye for colour, and much practice and experimenting.

Time spent practising colour mixing on a white tile will in the end be well worthwhile.

First steps in painting

Your restoration should be thoroughly clean and grease, excess adhesive and finger marks should be removed. Put a small amount of Solvol Autosol on a piece of rag and rub it over the piece, finally buffing it up to a nice clean surface ready for painting.

Ladle out a small quantity of Humbrol Enamel from the tin on to a clean white tile. Do not forget to re-seal the tin as soon as you have taken out the required amount of paint, as the paint will soon harden if left exposed to the air.

If the colour is not right, ladle out on to the tile, in separate pools, small quantities of the colours you think will shade it to the tone you require.

With a clean brush, draw a small amount from each pool of colour and mix together. In this way you can work slowly, making more separate pools, until you get a good matching colour.

You will find arriving at the right shade is a gradual process. The addition of a little black will darken the tone and white will lighten the tone. It is quite permissible, when you think you have achieved the correct matching colour, to dab it on to the surface of the china adjacent to the area to be painted, but not directly on to the area to be painted. The dab of paint should blend so well that it is difficult to distinguish. These testing dabs are easily removed with thinners or white spirit.

A base undercoat of white should be applied first. This should obliterate the repaired area. The next coat should match the ground colour of the china as nearly as possible, and then subsequent applications should be built up until the colour is an exact match. Each coat should be thoroughly dry before the next one is applied. Gently brush over with very fine abrasive paper before applying each following coat.

It is not always necessary to use glaze with Humbrol Enamel as it is with powder pigments. Depending on the gloss on the piece each coat of pigment can be progressively mixed with glaze ending with a final coat of almost pure glaze.

There is no limit to the number of coats that can be applied.

Apply the paint with bold, even, firm strokes over the entire area of repair. When you come to the edge of the repair you must graduate the paint so that the repaired area blends with the undamaged surface as invisibly as possible. Do not extend the paint too far on to the undamaged china. It is most important to avoid building up a ridge where the repaired area joins the undamaged part of the piece. This is quite a difficult process and needs a good deal of practice. The paint must be feathered out over the edges where the repair joins the original china.

The best way to do this, having covered the whole of the repaired area with paint, is to clean the brush with a clean cloth and apply the almost dry brush to the edges of the painted area. This will help to absorb the paint which has collected in a ridge where the repair joins the undamaged area.

Next, with a clean brush, mix paint with a small amount of thinner or white spirit and gently feather out over edges once more. Do not overload the brush. Repeat with the clean, almost dry, brush as before, and continue repeating the whole process until the painted area has merged with the undamaged glazed surface and completely disappeared.

The feathering process requires the lightest touch. It is a tricky process needing much practice. The smaller the amount of pigment used with the medium the easier it will be to feather out. Sometimes smudging the edges with your finger or with a silk rag will help to fade out the paint at the edges.

Decoration

You should only proceed on to the decoration when the ground colour has been thoroughly matched and blended with the undamaged area and is completely dry. Decorations on ceramics are seldom simple and your work will need to imitate the style of the original decorators. Designs are usually repetitive and incorporate complicated geometrical designs, flowers, foliage or figures.

The design can be lightly sketched in with an H pencil and a pair of dividers will be helpful in measuring out a repetitive pattern. A pattern usually has a main theme or feature, perhaps a garland, a circle or a specially positioned line or flower, and this will occur at regular intervals. With your dividers measure out the correct intervals, taking this feature as the key. With accurate measurements, your special line or shape will appear in the correct spacings across the repaired area finally matching up with the original pattern. Little dots of paint can be made to mark out where special features in the pattern should fall.

Another method is to trace the design from the undamaged part of the piece of china you are repairing, which will roughly match up and blend with the general design of the decoration. If you are fortunate enough to have a pair or a similar piece you can take your tracing from this.

Trace the pattern through fine tracing paper. With a soft pencil gently rub the back of the tracing paper, transferring the design on to a piece of thin white paper. This paper is, in turn, reversed and placed on to the repaired area, already painted in ground colour. The back of the paper is rubbed to impress the design on to the painted surface.

This may not give a clear facsimile of the design but it will give a rough outline and the missing lines can be filled in. Once the design has been sketched in it can be finely painted in a thin but strongly pigmented paint. Take care not to have a build-up of paint over the patterned area. Finely pointed brushes of varying sizes will be needed when applying the decoration.

Each colour should be completely dry before you apply the next colour, if there are many colours in the pattern.

Crazing or a tracery of cracks in the surface of the glaze, such as those frequently found in Staffordshire pottery and porcelain, can be copied by using a sharp pencil or a fine pointed brush dipped in the required colour.

For the crackle effect found in Chinese porcelain such as Celadon ware, a sharp pencil can be used to draw out the lines or a very fine pointed brush dipped in strong thin paint pigment. Carefully paint in the fine lines of the crackle and end with a coat of glaze, when the lines are quite dry. It is advisable to practise the crazing and crackle effects by drawing the lines out on paper or painting them on a bit of card or tile so as to achieve the easy flow of the lines. Put a piece of tracing paper over the crackle or crazing and let your pencil follow the lines to help you get the right directional flow.

Do not remove mistakes with thinners or solvent. It is safer to rub a mistake away with fine abrasive paper, as the use of thinners can remove the previous coats of paint and pattern.

Other cold setting paints and glazes

Chinaglaze (previously known as Pheenalite G310) is a two-pack urea formaldehyde/melamine formaldehyde substance which produces a hard heat-resisting lacquer. It is obtainable in clear gloss or satin.

For air-drying, Chinaglaze must be mixed with its catalyst in the proportion of 4 volumes base to 1 volume catalyst. Use a glass or polythene mixing container. In the beginning the liquid will be opaque, but continue mixing until a light clear solution is obtained. This mixture can be thinned with Phenthin 83. Care should be taken not to use too much thinner. The proportion of thinner to the mixture should be no more than 10% and considerably less if you are using Chinaglaze with Humbrol enamels. The glaze should be touch dry at room temperature in 40 minutes and completely dry in 2 to 3 hours.

Chinaglaze White is a specially formulated two-pack acid-cured lacquer with a matt white finish. It is very useful as the ground colour for porcelain or as a matt base coat. It may be necessary to cover the Chinaglaze white with an overcoat of Chinaglaze clear glaze to impart an extra gloss, in which case proceed as above.

Before applying Chinaglaze Gloss, Satin or White, make sure that the ceramic surface is absolutely clean and free of dust.

Do not use any of the mixed Chinaglaze Satin, Gloss or White after 24 hours. It should be discarded and a fresh mixture made up. All utensils should be cleaned with Phenthin 83.

Chinaglaze White can be thinned with Phenthin 83 using not more than 10% thinner. It should be touch dry in 40 minutes.

Good quality artists' powdered pigment

Powdered pigments can be mixed with Rustins Clear Gloss, Barbola Varnish, Rowney's Picture Varnish 800 or Chinaglaze with catalyst (mixed in the proportion of 4 parts to 1 part catalyst).

The powders are available from all art stores or Winsor and Newton (see list of suppliers, page 129). The advantage of this medium is its wide range of colours from which to choose. The colours can be obtained in small quantities, in packs of about 28 g (1 oz) and they last a considerable time as only very small amounts are used for mixing up the colours.

Select colours suitable for the work in hand. If several colours are needed put each colour on a large white tile. The powder paint is very light and fine so keep away from draughts and avoid breathing heavily over it as the particles will blow about. Put a small amount of varnish into a mixing saucer. Mix into the glaze the required pigment powder. A good deal of blending will be required to get all the grains of pigment smoothly and thoroughly blended with the glaze. Start with the smallest amount of glaze and increase the amount to adjust the density of colour.

You must be absolutely sure that no lumps are left in the mixture and that it is completely smooth before you start painting.

It will be necessary to estimate correct density and shade in mixing, it is therefore advisable to mix each colour with the glaze in separate mixing saucers so that you can judge the strength of each pigment and the amount that will be required. You will most likely find that you will have to add a little thinner to the mixture.

Artists' oil paints

Good quality artists' oil paints can be used very successfully on ceramics. They are probably easier to use than the powdered pigments, as they do not require the amount of grinding and mixing that is needed in blending the powdered pigments with their medium. Rustins Clear Gloss, Rowney's Picture Varnish 800, Barbola Varnish, and Chinaglaze Gloss can all be used as the medium with which to mix the oil paints. However, when not stoved these paints can take a very long time to dry, and the oil in the pigment makes it difficult to apply to ceramics. One way to overcome this problem is to squeeze out a little of each colour on to a piece of absorbent paper (not blotting or kitchen paper as these will leave small bits of fluff in the paint). Cover the squeezed-out paint for about twelve hours, after which the oil will have been absorbed into the paper and the pigment will be drier and easier to handle for retouching and painting ceramics. The disadvantage of this method is that you have to plan your colour mixing and matching well in advance, and be sure that you are going to be able to take up the work on that particular piece before the oil paint gets too dried out.

Mix the now oil-free pigment with the selected glaze medium. The application techniques for painting with artists' oils in the tubes or as powdered pigments remains the same as described for Humbrol Enamels.

On ceramics which have a dull matt surface Cryla paints can be used. These are paints which should be mixed with water. They can be obtained in a wide variety of colours, they dry quickly and are useful in the retouching of Wedgwood, terracota and ceramics with a matt surface.

Stoving paints

Chintex

This is a paint specially manufactured for use on ceramics. Chintex supply their own glaze and thinner and there is a wide choice of colours. Acetone and amylacetate are good solvents for Chintex paints. There is a Chintex Glaze Thinner as well as the paint thinner and this can also be used effectively as a solvent. The same technique is used to paint with Chintex paints as previously described for Humbrol Enamels, only it will be necessary to work more quickly, as the paint is thicker and tends to get tacky rather rapidly, especially if you are working in a warm atmosphere. The feathering process is also a little more difficult, owing to the bulky nature of the paint.

An application of pure clear Chintex Glaze on to the repaired surface, followed by stoving in an oven at a temperature of 104°C (220°F) for about 30–40 minutes will provide a smooth base for the opaque first coat. However, care must be taken here to prevent the Chintex Glaze from forming bubbles. It does have a tendency to do this, so make sure it does not collect in any crevices or hollows as this will encourage it to bubble during baking. If air bubbles have formed and burst during baking, leaving tiny holes in the glaze, drop a small quantity of glaze medium into the holes while the piece is still warm but not hot. This can be done with a fine paint brush or cocktail stick. The glaze should be absorbed into the holes. The piece may then be baked again or a further coat of glaze can be applied to the entire area, and baked, when the holes should have completely disappeared. Chintex paints can be stoved in a small table top electric oven which must be spotlessly clean and kept solely for the purpose of china restoration.

Never put the ceramic in a hot oven. Place the piece in a cool oven and let it slowly warm up to the required temperature; always let the oven cool down once more before removing the piece. If you remove the ceramic from a hot oven the sudden change in temperature can cause it to crack and break. Therefore after the usual baking period of approximately 30 minutes turn the oven off and wait at least 20 minutes before taking the china from the oven.

Always have several thick cloths handy for removing the china in case it is still warm and slips from your hands.

Stoving temperatures are as follows: 104°C (220°F) for 30–40 minutes for each coat of Chintex paint; 94°C (200°F) for 1 hour for the final coat of glaze.

Each coat of paint should be lightly rubbed down with fine abrasive paper before the next coat is applied, and each coat must be stoved.

Artists' oils from tubes, mixed with Chintex Glaze, can be stoved and the procedure is exactly the same as that described for painting with Chintex paints.

Chinaglaze (formerly Pheenalite G310) Satin and White can be stoved, and in this case you do not use the catalyst. The ceramic is stoved at a low temperature – 50°C (120°F) for 1½ hours or at 70°C (160°F) for 1 hour. As with Chintex paints, always put the ceramic in a cool oven and raise the temperature. After 1 hour or 1½ hours turn off the cooker and allow to cool before removing the piece from the oven. You should take very great care in stoving Chinaglaze because of its highly inflammable nature. Since it can be used very effectively with a catalyst in the cold method, it is not greatly recommended as a stoving paint.

China glaze must not be exposed near a naked flame

Summary of techniques in painting

Cold method (air-drying)
a Use Humbrol Enamels with Rustin's Clear Gloss, Humbrol Gloss, Rowney's Picture Varnish 800 or Chinaglaze with catalyst.
b Artists' Powdered Pigments with Rustin's Clear Gloss, Rowney's Picture Varnish 800, Barbola Varnish or Chinaglaze and catalyst.
c Artists' Oil Paints in tubes with Rustin's Clear Gloss, Rowney's Picture Varnish 800, Barbola Varnish or Chinaglaze with catalyst.

Hot method (stoving or baking)
a Chintex Paints with Chintex Glaze Medium
b Artists' Oils in tubes with Chintex Glaze or Chinaglaze

1. Practise on tiles in order to master the technique of brush work and mixing paints and colours.
2. The first layer should be quite opaque – usually a pure white base coat which will obliterate the repaired surface.
3. The ground colour is built up using less and less white and more colour pigment with each coat. If used with glaze medium, the amount of colour pigment should be decreased with each coat ending with a pure glaze coat or only slightly tinted glaze coat.
4. Each coat should be lightly rubbed with fine

abrasive paper before you apply the next coat.

5. Each coat must be absolutely dry before you rub it down and apply the following coat.

6. Paint on the undamaged area as little as possible.

7. Practise feathering out on a tile.

8. When stoving paints, baking time is 30 minutes plus approximately 20 minutes on either side for heating up and cooling down. Stoving temperatures are:

  For Chintex: 104°C (220°F) for 30-40 minutes
  For Chintex Glaze: 94°C (200°F) for 1 hour
  For Chinaglaze: 50°C (120°F) for 1½ hours
  70°C (160°F) for 1 hour

9. Never put china pieces into a hot oven or remove them directly from a hot oven.

Hints on matching paints

Matching colours in china ware is largely a matter of practice and an eye for colour, but the following hints may prove useful guidelines.

Flesh Tints White plus a touch of Paynes grey, Naples yellow, light red or burnt sienna.

Blue Delft Cobalt blue with a touch of black, brown or green.

Red Delft Alizarin crimson and light red with a touch of cobalt blue.

White Porcelain Matching white porcelain is not at all easy as there is such a tremendous range of tones in white and cream. The addition of Paynes grey, cerulean blue, cobalt blue, chrome green, raw umber or yellow ochre may be necessary. You can very rarely match white porcelain directly from the pot or tube.

Dark Blue (as in Worcester china) Ultramarine blue plus a little crimson lake or alizarin crimson.

Blues in oriental china Cobalt blue plus a touch of dark brown or green.

Reds in oriental china Cadmium red plus a touch of burnt sienna or burnt umber.

Matt surfaces Pigment mixed with a little varnish, to which is added a few flecks of talc powder, can achieve an effective matt surface. Otherwise use matt paints (Humbrol have a fairly wide range).

Unglazed wares (e.g. Wedgwood) Blend colours with resin composition or retouch with Cryla Paints.

To reduce brightness of colour Add burnt sienna, Paynes grey or raw umber.

Keep notes in your notebook as to the type of porcelain and the colours used.

Do not mix or match colours in an artificial light. Wait for daylight. The difference in matching is quite considerable especially with blues.

When you are working on a large piece of porcelain requiring several coats of the same colour it is a good idea to mix up a large quantity of the tone required – and when you have to pause before proceeding with the painting (overnight for instance) put the mixture in a small airtight bottle. This can be set aside and later thinned or colour-adjusted as necessary when you resume painting.

Keep all utensils and work surfaces very clean. Always clean the brushes immediately after use.

Keep your workbench as free as possible of clutter and always put lids and stoppers back on bottles and jars and screw up paint tubes immediately after use.

Chinaglaze with catalyst
Bronze powders
Red pigment
Cocktail sticks
Silk rags
Scissors
Mixing saucers
Palette knife
Methylated spirits
White spirit or turpentine
Acetone
Special sable brush for gilding
Agate burnisher

Gilding

Materials required for gilding

Treasure Gold liquid leaf
Tablet gold
Gold leaf
Bronze powders
Chintex glaze
Japlac
Humbrol varnish
Rustin's clear glaze

Gilding is usually the very last stage in restoring a piece of china. After retouching the decoration and applying a final coat of glaze, you will frequently be required to fill in some missing gold decoration. Usually the amount of gold decoration to be replaced is not very much, but the difficulty arises in matching the various shades and tones. It is surprising how many shades and colours of gold one encounters on various pieces of porcelain that are received for repair.

There are several different kinds of gold paint to be found but Treasure Gold Liquid Leaf is to be had in several different shades. It is easy to apply

90

and recommended for china restoration, especially for beginners. Liquid Leaf does, however, lack the lustre of Gold Leaf or Tablet Gold. In Liquid Leaf, Classic or Renaissance are good, general purpose colours. They can be applied straight from the bottle with a fine pointed brush kept solely for gilding. Turpentine is the usual solvent used for gold paint.

Bronze and gold powders Care must be exercised when using these powders as they are usually coarse textured, and very thorough mixing with the glaze medium is necessary. Bronze powders tend to discolour with age and will need to be finished with a protective coat of glaze medium. Bronze powders can be mixed with a polyurethane glaze, but care should be taken to use the same glaze medium as has been used in the rest of the painting. You are recommended to stove the final coat of glaze over the bronze powder, so if you are using a bronze powder as the gilding agent, stoving paints should be used in the rest of the decoration.

Gold leaf Gold leaf is possibly the most suitable medium for matching gold decoration for china. It is obtainable in booklets of small sheets backed by tissue paper, which take a good deal of the strain out of handling, as you will usually have to cut out rather small and fiddly patterns or fine strips.

The area to be decorated must, as in all painting, be absolutely clean and free of dust and other particles.

Gold leaf needs a size in order for it to adhere to the porcelain. The medium used is usually Japlac, Rustin's Clear Glaze or Chinaglaze plus catalyst (if you are not stoving).

The design must be painted in the glaze medium, and this should be tinted so that it can be easily seen. A little red pigment is usually added to the glaze. The glaze must be fairly thin so as not to form a raised ridge along the decoration.

Pour a little glaze into a mixing bowl and mix with a little red pigment.

Draw in the lines of the pattern with a soft pencil. Then paint over these lines with a very fine pointed sable brush which has been dipped in the glaze and red pigment mixture. Make the design a fraction smaller than the original, and overlap on to the pattern a little way at each end.

Leave this to become just tacky to the touch, about 15 minutes. If you are using Chintex Glaze and stoving it will be a little longer.

Cut out the pattern in gold leaf. Having made sure that the glaze has just begun to get tacky, lay the pattern quickly over the glaze, tissue side up.

Carefully rub your finger or a wooden tool lightly over the pattern, and gently lift the tissue away from the gold leaf. At this stage you may be disappointed to find you have not got a good clean unblemished facsimile of the design in gold, but do not despair, this is not unusual. There are always some ragged edges and places where the gold has failed to adhere. Remove the loose bits with a soft brush and use a wet cocktail stick to coax the remaining ragged edges into place.

If necessary, another coat of gold can be applied. This should be laid on the first layer as quickly as possible, without the addition of another layer of glaze.

Cut out the corrective second pattern and lay it on to the first layer, then gently rub it and lift the tissue. In all probability all that will be necessary now is a little more light brushing to remove the loose bits of gold. However, if it is still a little ragged, you will have to make a third application, and this time you will have to apply another line of glaze over the pattern as you did with the first application. However, you should avoid applying two layers of glaze if possible as this will create a ridge and raise the decoration above the level of the surface of the ceramic, when it should be flush with the surface.

If you are using Chintex as a glaze medium, stoving will be necessary. Note that with air-drying clear varnish or Chinaglaze with catalyst stoving is unnecessary.

When *absolutely* dry the gold leaf should be burnished with an agate burnisher. This is a small, delicately shaped, fragile tool. Rub it in a gentle circular motion directly on the gold leaf to bring the gold leaf up to the desired lustre. This tool should be stored away carefully as it is expensive and easily destroyed.

Apply a final protective clear glaze coating.

Tablet gold Tablet gold is very expensive and should not be used when a large amount of gold decoration needs replacing, as this will make your repair very costly. Apply the gold with a fine brush dipped in water – use the smallest amount of water. Pull the brush over the tablet, loading on gold as it travels along. You will have to use a stippling action in applying tablet gold, i.e. dab the area to be gilded with the point of your brush. Do not use strokes when applying tablet gold. Leave to dry for at least 24 hours. If the gold adheres well when gently touched, you can safely burnish with your agate burnisher. In some cases it may be necessary to apply several coats and the procedure is repeated. Finish with a final protective coat of clear glaze. Again if using Chintex you will have to stove the work for the usual time and at the usual temperature.

Tablet gold can be reused if the brush is dipped in a little water so do not wash the brush after use, but leave whatever gold powder is remaining on it, to dry and put it aside for further use.

Summary of points to be observed when gilding

With gold leaf
1. Brush and ceramic should be free of all dust and fluff and completely dry.
2. Mix size with small amount of pigment.
3. Cut leaf into required strips for pattern.
4. Paint in lines of pattern with tinted glaze and leave to dry until just tacky.
5. When tacky, apply gold leaf.
6. Clean loose bits away with soft brush, and trim design edges with wet cocktail stick.
7. Burnish when absolutely dry.
8. Apply final coat of clear glaze (either air-drying varnish or stoving varnish).

With tablet gold
1. Clean china and brush thoroughly.
2. Dip fine brush in water and draw over tablet.
3. Stipple design on to porcelain.
4. When quite dry, burnish.
5. Apply protective coat of clear glaze.
6. Do not wash gold powder off brush – leave for reuse.

With bronze or gold powders
1. Mix very thoroughly with glaze medium.
2. Finish with protective coat of glaze medium.
3. The final coat of glaze over bronze powders should be stoved.

Always have a separate brush for gilding, and never apply other paint pigments to china with the brush you use for gilding.

———————————

—8. THE USE OF THE AIRBRUSH—

Materials required

Tools
Airbrush (see list on page 100)
Compressor and ancillary
  equipment (pressure gauge,
  moisture extractor)
Stiff bristle brush
Magnifying glass

Materials
Paints and solvents (chapter 7)
Acetone
Solvol Autosol polish

General equipment
Various glass containers with

metal screw tops
Plain white and plain black or
  brown tiles
White absorbent kitchen paper
Clean silk or cotton cloths
Wooden cocktail sticks
Mixing saucers

Large areas of restoration on ceramics can be painted with very satisfactory results by means of an airbrush. When the repaired area is very large it is not practical and indeed is very difficult to achieve a good smooth finish with hand painting.

There are many good airbrushes from which to choose, but when buying an airbrush, you should aim to get one that is easy to clean, as this is a most important factor in the use of any airbrush. Even the tiniest particle of paint or glaze left in the airbrush to dry will block the small air passage, and this will make your work tedious and slow down progress enormously. It is very exasperating and

often quite disastrous to find splodges of paint suddenly appearing on your repair.

The paint should flow through in a fine smooth spray and difficulties such as a sudden burst of too much paint or a fine granular speckling appearing when it should not, can all be avoided with careful cleaning and treatment of the airbrush.

In addition to the airbrush, a compressor will be necessary, as the airbrush works on the principle that air is forced through the body of the instrument under pressure of 20–30 lbs per square inch –psi (2·76mks to 4·14mks). The air passes out of the airbrush through a small hole at the end of a nozzle in the front. Paint is introduced into the airflow when a valve at the back of the nozzle is opened by pulling back a trigger or lever which operates the needle. This is a long fine metal object which runs along the interior of the airbrush. When the paint control lever is pulled back the needle is drawn away from the aperture at the front of the airbrush, allowing paint to flow through. The paint in the paint cup is drawn up and into the airflow, past the needle. It mixes with the air and comes out of the hole at the end of the nozzle at the front in a fine atomized spray. Some airbrushes are regulated by an up and down movement of the finger on the paint release lever, while others operate with a backwards and forwards movement on the trigger. Detailed instructions come with the instruments, however, the principle is the same in each case.

Most airbrush dealers supply their own compressors in conjunction with the airbrush (see list of tools and materials). However, you must be sure that the compressor is the correct type for your airbrush, and supplies the correct pressure per pound. A pressure gauge and a moisture extractor are very useful and necessary additions to the smooth untroubled operation of the airbrush. The aerosol cans which can be used with airbrushes are not very practical in the long term.

Airbrush painting requires a good deal of practice before one can be really proficient in its use. It is therefore advisable to devote a considerable time to practising spray painting on plain ceramic tiles before working on a repair.

Method

Spoon a small amount of Humbrol Enamel paint, mixed with a little thinner, into a small clean container. You may take the paint out with a brush or pour it directly into the colour cup from the tin, but as you will later be mixing and matching colours when you paint on to ceramics, the small metal screw tops to bottles are very useful for mixing up the colours into the correct matching tones. If you use a brush to remove the paint from the tin be sure there are no loose hairs or fluff on the brush which could escape into the paint.

Start practising a few simple exercises. Make small dots on your tile in pencil or in paint with a fine pointed brush about 12 mm ($\frac{1}{2}$ in) apart. Now holding your airbrush 12 mm to 18 mm ($\frac{1}{2}$ to $\frac{3}{4}$ in) away from the tile try spraying dots on to the dots you have marked on the tile. This will give you good practice in the finger-tip control necessary in airbrushing. Repeat the process, gradually enlarging the dots by allowing more paint to flow through the brush. You will soon discover the distances the brush should be held from the tile in order to enlarge the dots. If the airbrush is held too close to the tile, the dots will become shapeless blobs.

In using the airbrush you should work with a relaxed arm and wrist movement. With another clean tile, start moving the airbrush from left to right, but do not let any colour flow through at first. Gradually let the flow start at the point you plan will be the beginning of a line on your tile, continue along the line and stop the flow of paint at the point you wish to be the end of your line. However, do not stop your hand movement abruptly but continue moving the airbrush although you have lifted your finger off the paint release lever and stopped the flow of colour.

Practise this movement on a tile or a sheet of paper. A tile is a more suitable surface because whereas a strong spray of paint will be absorbed into paper it will tend to flow down the smooth ceramic surface of the tile. Use of a tile therefore allows you to judge the strength and size of the spray line more realistically.

When you are thoroughly at home with the movement and can achieve a good fine line, you can start to practise widening the line by allowing more colour to flow and increasing the distance of the airbrush from the tile surface.

Start a fine line and widen it at the end by pulling the airbrush up and away from the surface as you move along. Remember always to keep the airbrush moving even after the paint flow has been cut off. A good deal of practise at this is necessary to achieve a light lever control and become relaxed in handling the airbrush.

Having practised thoroughly and gained some proficiency and confidence, you can now try your hand at spray painting on to a ceramic. Do not start on an important piece. Early spray painting should be carried out on old unimportant pieces on which you should put in as much practise as possible. These early stages of practise are most important and should not be neglected. All the paints described in the chapter on painting, with the exception of Cryla paints, can be put through the airbrush. The glazes, especially Chinaglaze, must be thinned with the appropriate thinners. When using powdered pigments and glaze medium be sure to mix the powder and glaze together very thoroughly, grinding and blending them to a smooth grain-free liquid, as the smallest grain of powder will clog the airbrush and prevent a smooth flow of paint, or even stop it altogether.

Using the relaxed arm and wrist movement as described, spray the paint in parallel lines from left to right and right to left, each line slightly overlapping the previous one. The spraybrush can also be used in a circular movement, but always be sure the lines overlap each other a fraction.

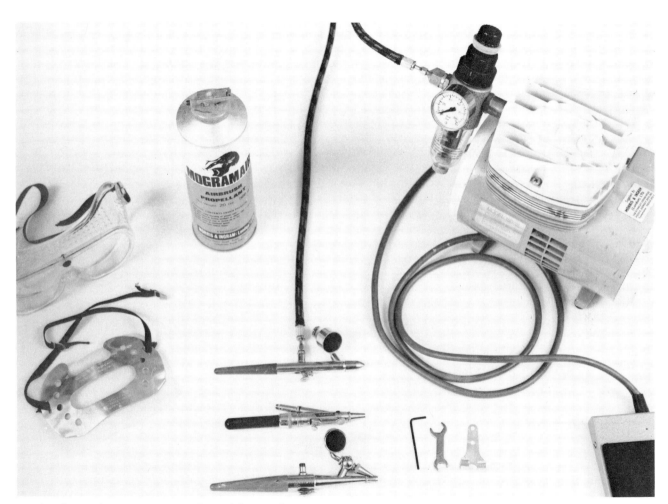

Air brushes with compressor, goggles and face mask

Always keep the airbrush moving as just one stationary moment over a particular spot will produce a puddle of paint. As with hand painting, several layers of paint can be applied, each layer having less pigment and more glaze so that you end up with a final layer of pure glaze, thinned sufficiently to flow easily through the fine nozzle. Again, as in hand painting, each layer should be lightly rubbed with a fine abrasive paper before applying the next coat. Also each coat should be thoroughly dry before the next coat is applied. Avoid painting over on to the undamaged glaze, as much as possible.

Shading

This is achieved with an airbrush by first spraying the darker denser colour, then drawing the airbrush up and away from the surface in order to lighten the tone. The distance between the airbrush and the surface will regulate the density of the tone.

Speckling

This can be achieved by means of a spatter cup usually supplied with the airbrush.

Cleaning

Always clean the airbrush *immediately* after use and never leave it standing with the paint or glaze in it for more than a few seconds. Remove the paint cup and spray out the residue of paint. Fill and clean the paint cup with solvent. Spray solvent through the brush from the cleaned paint cup; while spraying cover the nozzle in front of the airbrush with your finger so that the solvent blows back into the cup. Repeat this procedure several times.

When you have finished all your spray painting for the day, before putting the airbrush away be sure that it is completely free of all paint particles which, if left to dry, will clog the fine passages. Clean with the same solvent that you have been using for the paint and glaze. Keep spraying the solvent through the brush until it comes through absolutely clean and clear and without the slightest tinge of colour. It may be necessary to remove the needle and this should be done with the utmost care as the fine tip of the needle can be very easily bent. A bent needle can cause endless problems with the spray, such as blotching and spattering. Do not dismantle the spray gun unless you are quite sure that you can successfully get it together again.

Clean the nozzle and sprayhead thoroughly with a stiff bristle brush dipped in solvent. *Never poke sharp pointed metal objects into any parts of the airbrush in order to clean it. If there appears to be some particle of paint which won't move, a cocktail stick dipped in acetone and gently pushed and worked against the offending particle so as to dislodge it is all the probing permitted.

Make sure that all the colour cups are clean of all paint and the solvent flows clearly and freely through the narrow connecting tube.

Examine your airbrush through a magnifying glass, and do not put it away until you are quite satisfied that it is absolutely clean and not the smallest particle of paint remains. If you are going to use the brush within the next few days you may leave it with the nozzle and sprayhead immersed in a jar of white spirit. Make sure that the needle is retracted and the tip is not pressing against the bottom or sides of the container.

Problems

The most common problem encountered when using the airbrush is caused by small particles of dried paint either on the needle or in the sprayhead nozzle clogging the air passages and interfering with the smooth flow of paint. Therefore be absolutely meticulous in always seeing that your airbrush and its colour cups are spotlessly clean. There is nothing that tries the patience more than settling down to painting with the airbrush, only to find that you have to spend precious time dismantling it to clean out old paint that has been left to dry and clog the brush. Airbrushing can, in time, facilitate the painting of restored ceramics and speed up the work considerably, but it will require plenty of patience and practice in the early stages. If thorough cleaning is neglected, it will do just the reverse and slow your work down considerably.

Blotching
The brush is being held too close to the work.

Overspray
A hazy matt area appears along the edges of the painted surface. This is more apparent on highly glazed ceramics. This matt surround is caused in most cases by incorrect air pressure. Remember 20-30 psi (2·76-4·14 mks) is the usual air pressure required in painting on ceramics.

If the glaze mixture is too thick, overspray can result.

Splattering
This can be caused by:
1. A badly ground pigment. Check the mixture and see that the pigments are thoroughly ground, leaving the mixture smooth and free of the minutest grain. See that there are no fluff or dust particles in the paint mixture.
2. A bent needle.
3. Dirt in the airbrush. Inspect the airbrush thoroughly through a magnifying glass. Look out for fluff or old dried paint which may be blocking the air passages.

4. Check your air pressure. It could be too low.

Orange peeling

When the paint does not settle on the surface of the ceramic smoothly and evenly but has a rough pitted appearance similar to that of orange peel, the paint is probably too thick. For airbrushing, the consistency of the paint should be rather like that of milk in order for it to flow smoothly through the nozzle. If the air pressure is too high, orange peeling can result, so check the air pressure on your pressure gauge.

Finishing off:

When the final coat of glaze is absolutely dry you may want to adjust the depth of gloss to a more or less shiny surface. To increase the gloss, put a small amount of Solvol Autosol on to a clean cloth, and with the reverse side of the cloth polish very gently, checking frequently until you have arrived at the correct gloss finish. In order to reduce the amount of gloss squeeze a small amount of Simoniz Car Polish on to a clean damp rag and gently polish. Do not over-polish as you are aiming to match the repaired area with the original as nearly as possible, so keep checking during the polishing.

Points to be observed when painting with an airbrush

1. Keep the airbrush spotlessly clean at all times. *Never* put it away until all paint and glaze has been cleaned out with the appropriate solvent for the type of paint that you have been using. Never leave paint or glaze in the airbrush for more than a few minutes, and always flush out with solvent.

2. Let the air run through the airbrush before you start to paint, so as to expell any moisture that may have settled in the tube lines. A moisture extractor is useful for this purpose.
Spray a little solvent through the brush before you start to spray with paint pigment.

3. Have a colour cup set aside containing solvent so that after each colour has been sprayed it can be quickly cleaned out of the brush, before a new colour is introduced.

4. Paint can be blended to the required shade by mixing in a small container (the small screw tops to bottles are useful) until the correct tone is achieved. Then pour the paint into the colour cup for spraying on to the repair.

5. The paint should not be too thick. If necessary it should be thinned with the appropriate thinner. The consistency should be similar to that of milk.

6. The degree of the density of the tone depends on the distance the airbrush is held from the surface of the ceramic. The further the distance, the lighter the tone.
7. Keep the airbrush moving when the paint is flowing and overlap each line of paint.
8. Fine lines can be achieved by holding the paint release lever well forward so that the aperture through which the paint flows is small. Hold the brush fairly close to the surface of the ceramic.
9. Broad lines can be achieved by holding the paint release lever back, so that the opening through which the paint flows will be wide. Hold the brush further away from the surface of the ceramic.

Some types of airbrushes

Conopois
Fairly easy to clean, care must be taken not to bend the tip when removing the needle. This brush can be adjusted to a very fine spray line.
De Vilbiss Airbrush
Colour cup is attached. Fairly easy to clean. A good easy brush to regulate.
Badger Airbrush
Not very easy to clean. Remove needle with care, as it can be bent easily. A special brush for ceramics gives a good spray.
Paasche
A very good brush for cleaning. It will not be necessary to remove the needle with this airbrush too often but care should be taken when doing so. It is a little less delicate than in most.

---

9. THE REPAIR OF MISCELLANEOUS WARES

The restorer will frequently be brought wares other than ceramics to repair, and while the basic procedures for bonding and filling remain the same for all wares, the types of adhesives and materials for cleaning and filling for different wares are listed below.

Alabaster

Alabaster is a substance which resembles marble. It is used mainly for vases and statues. Modern alabaster is a sulphate of lime composition, and is soft and slightly soluble in water.

To clean Use white spirit, petrol or benzine. *Never* use water.

To bond Use polyvinyl acetate or Sintolit when the break is large and a strong bond is required. If dowelling is necessary, use stainless steel dowels.

To fill 1. A filling made from microcrystalline wax, Cosmolloid 80H (Victory white) and Ketone N (polycyclohexanone resin used in varnish). The proportion of one part microcrystalline wax to two parts Ketone N must be very carefully heated, as this mixture is very inflammable. It is therefore advisable to heat over water in a double boiler, melting the mixture slowly. When the mixture has completely melted pour it on to a sheet of silicone paper, preferably in some sort of shallow container so that it will not flow off the paper. Allow to cool and apply the cold filling into the cracks with a warmed modelling tool. Smooth down the resin filling with a cloth dampened with white spirit. 2. Plaster of Paris mixed with melted beeswax. Melt the beeswax in a basin over hot water. Here, again, work with caution as beeswax is highly inflammable. Apply filling with heated modelling tool.

To retouch Use Cryla paints.

Glass

Glass is not an easy ware to repair. The smoothness of the break edges makes bonding quite difficult, and it is not possible to make a glass bond invisible.

To clean Wash with warm water and a good detergent. Bad stains and lime deposits can be removed by soaking in a solution of 5 parts sodium hydroxide to 1 part water. Rinse very thoroughly. Rinsing in a solution of household ammonia and warm water will also clean glass very effectively.

To bond Bond with two-tube Araldite (*Devcon Clear*) or AY103/HY956 (*Epotek 301 or RP103*). Because the break edges are usually smooth and slippery, they tend to slide about when brought together, and a perfect union is quite difficult to achieve. The bonding process can be simplified by roughening the edges with a diamond drill point.

To fill You are not recommended to fill large missing areas in glass. Most materials will discolour and it is rarely possible to get an invisible filling. For smaller cracks and chips and missing areas a methacrylate resin can be used (Plastogen G or *Clearcast*). Pour a small amount of Plastogen G into a container, add a small amount of hardener from the end of a spatula and mix together thoroughly.

Cover the container immediately and leave to stand for a few minutes. When all the air bubbles have escaped apply the Plastogen to the area to be filled with a spatula. Skin forms almost as soon as the Plastogen G has been applied and it cannot be worked once the skin has formed so it may be necessary to build the filling up in layers. Plastogen takes about half an hour to set. The missing area should be backed by adhesive tape or gumstrip before the resin is poured into the hole. The glass object should be balanced so that the resin sets level and does not trickle out of the hole.

Polyester casting resins can also be used for fillings. For coloured glass, oil pigment can be added to the polyester resin. This is not a very easy material to deal with and it is expensive.

One of the more usual breaks in glass ware is that of the stem from the bowl of the glass. Here a dowel can be used, if the stem and bowl are thick enough to withstand the drilling without shattering. A glass dowel of the appropriate size is used. The dowelling procedure is the same as for ceramics. Drill the holes, keeping the diamond head under water during drilling. Fill the holes with an Araldite mixture and apply Araldite to the break edges. Cut the dowel with a diamond cutting disc to the desired length, and insert it into the hole. Bring the two pieces together and strap them into place. It is usually more convenient to stand the glass on its rim for setting. Polish the glass with Solvol Autosol. Do not use abrasive papers on glass; chipped edges can be smoothed down by rubbing a dampened carborundum stone gently over the chipped edge until it is smooth.

Ivory

Ivory comes from the tusk of an elephant, and it is usually found, delicately carved, in oriental statues, ornaments, boxes and figurines. It is very brittle and must be handled with care.

To clean With white spirit. Never use water.

To bond Polyvinyl acetate emulsion (Evostick W).

To fill The fillings of cracks and missing pieces in ivory should be carried out by specialized craftsmen in this field.

Jade

A hard stone, the substance of which is silicate of lime and magnesia. Jade stone comes in colours ranging from cream to various shades of blue, yellow and green. It is used mainly by the Chinese to carve ornaments, bowls and cups. Early Chinese carvings on jade objects were rendered with the most amazing delicacy and beauty.

To clean Use distilled water.

To bond With AY103/HY956 (*Epotek 301 or RP103*).

To fill With AY103/HY956 to which is added a small amount of powdered pigment to match colour. If dowelling is necessary, glass dowels should be used.

Terracotta

Terracotta is a fired clay used for statues, figurines, bowls and vases. It is usually unglazed, although some objects are painted over and glazed. It is usually a reddish colour, but the tone varies from a very light, almost creamy yellow to a dark brick. It is a very porous substance.

To clean Wash in water, but do not leave it soaking in the water.

To bond With polyvinyl acetate emulsion or Sintolit.

To fill Polyfilla mixed with water to the correct consistency to which powdered pigment is added to match the tone of the pottery.

To retouch Cryla paints.

Marble

A crystalline limestone found mainly in architecture and in sculptures and statues. It can be carved with comparative ease and can be polished to a very high gloss.

To clean Care must be taken in cleaning marble. White marble can be washed with water and a good quality soap. Stains can be removed by the application of petrol, alcohol, benzine, acetone or a sepiolite mixture. Never use acids to clean marble, and never use water and soap on coloured marble.

To bond With Sintolit or polyvinyl acetate emulsion.

To fill A mixture of polyvinyl acetate emulsion and marble flour. If dowelling is necessary use stainless steel dowels, and remember not to use metal tools with polyvinyl acetate emulsion.

10. HOBBY OR BUSINESS

It will not be long before it becomes known that you are mending china and you will soon have a stream of friends and neighbours at your door, with their precious pieces for you to repair. At this point you will need to make the decision whether you want to restore china as a hobby or go into the restoration of ceramics as a business. However, either as a hobby or as a business, restoring china can be profitable.

China restoration as a hobby

If you decide that you do not want to become involved in the complicated world of business but simply want to restore ceramics for your own pleasure, you will find plenty to keep you busy and interested. You may well find yourself becoming quite an addict for jumble sales where there are usually pieces in need of restoration to be found on the stalls, which can be obtained for a very reasonable sum. Friends moving house are usually more than happy to pass on boxes of broken china,

unearthed in their packing up, or pieces broken in the move. Moving always seems to damage a few pieces and the unwanted ones can be very welcome in your workroom, often presenting you with something interesting and challenging to restore.

Auction rooms can also be a good source for finding ceramics in need of repair. Auctioneers make up 'job lots', i.e. boxes or baskets of odds and ends in which there are nearly always some damaged pieces of porcelain, and these 'lots' usually go for modest sums of money at the sales. Some auctioneers will let you go through their boxes of broken pieces considered too damaged to put in the sales, and these they will, in all probability, let you take away with no charge. So it is worth calling in on your local salerooms and getting to know the staff. Auctioneers are usually very busy people so do not choose a day when they are getting ready for their next sale or when goods are coming in for the sale. If you can select a time when they are not so busy you will find them most helpful.

In time you may decide to specialize in repairing

only a certain type of china, and so make up a small collection for yourself. You may find that you will want to put some of these in the sales yourself, and you will frequently be agreeably surprised at the cheque you receive for these repaired pieces.

Antique shops and good junk shops may also be interested in buying your excess repaired pieces. When putting your restored pieces into an auction sale you need not inform the auctioneer that they are restored pieces. It is for the dealers and buyers to find this out for themselves when they examine the pieces before the sale. However, when selling directly to an antique or a junk shop, you should point out that the pieces are restored and they should subsequently be sold as such.

These transactions will help to cover the cost of your materials and it is not unknown to find that one of the pieces repaired could be more valuable than estimated, bringing in a handsome windfall.

You will, of course, have friends bringing you their pieces to repair and you may be perfectly happy simply to indulge in your hobby and make no charge. However, they will probably want to reward you for your time and skill in returning their much loved ceramic to them, in one piece once more, in which case the cost of the materials would be a reasonable recompense, or you might suggest they give you the equivalent in materials or a small piece of equipment.

China-mending as a business

Should you decide that you want to go into mending china as a business it is advisable as a first step to seek the advice of experts, before you start acquiring premises and setting yourself up. There are many rules and regulations, for which the advice of a solicitor is necessary, and an accountant's help will be invaluable in the vexing problems of finances, taxation, etc.

In the beginning, you should 'start small'. If you are working from your home, check on the regulations with your local council. If you wish to rent premises visit an estate agent and explain your requirements to him. You will not want a large prestigious shop with shop front. A small back room is all that is necessary, provided it has the requisite light, storage and working space, electricity and plumbing. An advertisement in your local newspaper will frequently produce the right premises. Sometimes antique dealers have rooms at the back of their shops which they would be happy to rent out to a 'resident restorer'.

Having found your premises, your next step is to advertise; here again your local newspaper will be useful. Run your advertisement for several weeks or have it put in at regular intervals. The advertising departments of newspapers are very helpful in giving advice of this nature.

Printed postcards displayed in newsagents' windows are an inexpensive form of advertising, and a surprisingly good source of potential customers.

You should have some good business cards printed, including your name, address and telephone number and, of course, some indication that you repair ceramics, e.g.

Samuel Chamberlaine
Restorer of Fine Pottery and Porcelain
Tel. No.   Address

These you should distribute to your local antique dealers, good junk shops and shops selling china ware. Most departmental stores selling china are not interested in the restorer, as broken pieces of modern tea, coffee, and dinner sets are usually sent back to the factories, the stores and manufacturers being covered by insurance, and they therefore do not need the restorer's services.

It is a good idea to get a list of antique fairs to be held in your area and if you can spare the time, rent a stall. Have a few examples of your work during the various stages of repair on display. This is always a draw, as people will drift over to examine the work and question you on how you go about restoring certain wares. Have some restored pieces for sale, and do not forget to have your cards put out in a conspicuous position.

Hints on how to conduct your business

It is a golden rule that you should give a rough estimate of the cost on receipt of the article brought to you for repair. It will, therefore, be necessary for you to learn to make quick assessments of costs. Try to make a point of strapping up the broken pieces brought to you in the presence of your customer; when there are too many pieces to do this within a reasonable time, strap the pieces up in the 'dry run' as soon as you can, and immediately follow it up with a written estimate. When giving rough estimates, on receipt of the article, explain to the customer that as the work proceeds unforeseen difficulties can arise and you are now giving only an approximate estimate. In the event of extensive unexpected difficulties arising which will increase the cost, you should get in touch immediately with your customer and discuss the difficulty and increased costs before proceeding with the work.

The value of the 'dry run' can now be seen, for by strapping up the article on receipt you will be able to judge to some degree the extent of the repair. Often, what looks like a simple bonding job proves to be otherwise when all the pieces are assembled; you may find the work will involve making up and replacing missing pieces. You will sometimes be presented with a carefully made up parcel of broken pieces, and be told 'we gathered up all the bits, even the tiniest pieces,' when in fact a couple of quite large pieces or chips escaped notice and got swept away. Only by strapping up do you find that they are missing. The importance of doing this strapping up of the broken pieces in the presence of your customer cannot be stressed too much.

Most people have no idea how long it takes to mend a piece of porcelain, and in the beginning, you will naturally be slower than when you have gained more experience and expertise. China restoration is a slow process if it is done well – the removal of stains alone can take several weeks, filling, rubbing, painting and drying all take considerable time and researching can take many months. When you have several pieces on which to work, you will find the time factor quite a problem, especially if you are working on your own. So do not fail to warn your customer that repairing takes time, and give yourself a good long period in which to do the work if you are asked to give a date of completion. Work will suffer if you are pressurized.

Keep the pieces that are waiting to be repaired all together in a cupboard or on a shelf on one side. Put each piece to be repaired into a box or bag, with all its loose pieces in an envelope or packet attached and clearly marked. The repaired items awaiting collection should be kept together on another shelf set aside specially for completed pieces.

Have cards printed to send out reminding your customers that their articles are complete and now ready for collection. You may have to remind some customers several times to collect their completed items. Your business will not be very successful if, after many hours of work, pieces remain on your shelves uncollected for months or even years. So include in small print, on the bottom of your reminder cards, a notice saying that pieces left to be repaired and not collected after a certain time will be sold to defray costs.

As soon as you have received an article for repair, mark a number on the base in waterproof pencil or on a waterproof label and stick it on to the base of the piece. Enter that number in a ledger against which you should write the name of the owner and the description of the article and repair required, estimated cost and date completed (see specimen at the end of this section).

Try and avoid having to post repaired pieces to your customers. Make it a rule that pieces should be brought and collected personally. Have plenty of boxes, tissue paper, string, foam-rubber pieces and wood shavings for packing. If you have to dispatch a piece of china by post, or a customer requires a piece to be well packed before he takes it away, see that the object is wrapped in several layers of tissue paper. Fill the base of a good strong box of appropriate size with foam-rubber chips, wood shavings or vermiculite (as used in roof insulation) to the depth of about 25 mm (1 inch). Place the piece on this base and wrap any lids or separate pieces separately. Then fill the box with more foam-rubber, wood shavings or vermiculite. The object should have a good all-round clearance from the sides of the box; the packing material will fill in the space between the object and the sides of the box. Strap the box up well with brown paper, string and adhesive tape as appropriate. Mark the package FRAGILE WITH CARE. Never hammer nails into a box in which you have packed china. If you have had to use a wooden box, clip or screw the lid in place and remember not to pack the china too tightly in its container.

Costs and estimates

It is very difficult to be categorical about costs as there are no hard and fast rules on what should be charged to repair china.

Whatever method you decide to use in estimating fees always make your estimate higher than your first mental assessment. You invariably take longer than you imagine and, more often than not, run into unexpected difficulties, which inevitably slow you down and involve more work. It is not good policy, except in very rare instances, to come back to a client, having given a quotation, with a new and higher estimate when you find there is more work involved, so do take this into account when you estimate the cost of your work.

There are several methods by which to gauge your costs and it is left to the individual repairer to decide which is the most suitable. The methods of costing set out below, are, therefore, only guidelines.

Some restorers charge for their work on a time basis, i.e. they charge so much per hour. In the beginning you will be working slowly, so you can increase your hourly rate as you get more expert and your work speeds up. However, you will have to keep very careful time-sheets if using this method, remembering not to charge for the time when the adhesives and paints are drying and when the piece is soaking during the removal of stains, as you will be working on other pieces during these times. Customers usually like to be given quotations of what you are likely to charge when they leave the piece for repair, and this is not so easy to assess in the beginning, using this method of costing, for without the benefit of much experience you will not always know how long it might take you to complete a particular piece of work.

An easier method for giving quick estimates is to charge per broken piece. If a piece of porcelain broken into eight pieces is brought to you for repair, you can give a quick estimate by multiplying the sum you decide to charge per piece by eight and on to that you can add a percentage to cover making up and replacing missing pieces or any additional work.

You can estimate costs on the known value of the article, by simply charging a percentage of its value. You should, of course, try not to charge more for a repair than the intrinsic value of the piece. At times, however, this may not be possible; a piece may be brought to you which requires work far beyond its worth, but because of the sentimental value to the owner the high price will be paid for the repair. A list of charges for more usual repairs can be made and kept for guidance:

1. Simple bonds (2 pieces)
Cup
Saucer
Plate
Bowl

2. Bonds (2 pieces)
Removal of stains, breaking down of old repairs and rebonding
Cup
Saucer
Plate
Bowl

3. Multiple breaks: simple bond (3, 4, 5, etc. pieces)
Cup
Saucer
Plate
Bowl

4. Multiple breaks (3, 4, 5, 6, etc. pieces)
Breaking down old repairs, removal of stains, rebonding
Cup
Saucer
Plate
Bowl

5. Shell breaks

6. Building up and replacing missing pieces
Hands and fingers
Legs and feet
Arms and hands
Feet
Wings

7. Replacing handles

As you will be given such a variety of pieces to repair, and no two pieces are the same, no list can be completely comprehensive; you will constantly be adding to your list as new problems come your way, and it can become a helpful guide.

Always send written estimates of the repair, even if you have given a verbal assessment. It is not necessary to give a very detailed description of the work to be done, it is sufficient merely to state brief details of the piece and a short description of the work to be carried out. Have printed on your estimates wording to the effect that work left for you to repair will be given all care while it is in your possession, but that all pieces are left at the owner's risk, and you are not responsible for loss or damage. It is also as well to go into the question of insurance thoroughly with your solicitors.

There will inevitably be plenty of paper work to do when running a business. Apart from the tax forms and the work connected with the personal side of your business, there will be letters to write, estimates and orders to make and accounts to keep and you must be meticulous in keeping very accurate records. If you are not conversant with the art of book-keeping, seek the advice and guidance of someone who knows about such things.

You will need a large cash ledger open at a double page. On the left-hand page enter every item that you pay out in connection with your business; this includes everything from your rent and insurance down to the sugar and tea you buy for your tea break, as it is this total which is taken into account when your tax returns are being assessed. On the right-hand page enter every sum received. At the end of each month total up each side and deduct the smaller amount from the larger total. This calculation will reveal to you the amount of your profit or loss for the month. Usually in the beginning the total on the left-hand side (debit) of your ledger wi!l exceed the total on the right (credit). But this is not at all unusual and should not cause concern as in the early stages you will have had to pay for equipment in order to set yourself up. It will take some months for incoming funds to filter through to cover costs so that you can break even and eventually show a profit.

Your initial capital outlay for equipment and materials is relatively very small indeed and should not involve much more than the items listed below:

1. Airbrush, compressor and ancillary parts
2. Electric drill and drill points
3. De-ionizing unit
4. Small table-top electric cooker for stoving repairs
5. Office furniture: cupboards; workbench etc.
6. Tools and materials

The repair and restoration of porcelain is open

to all groups of people, the young and active, or those who, for some reason, are confined to the home, caring, perhaps, for an elderly or invalid relative, or because of disablement. There is no age limit, provided you are fairly deft with your fingers and your eyesight is still good. It is, therefore, eminently suitable for those who face retirement, not without misgivings as to the empty days of boredom which might lie ahead. Here is the answer, a hobby or a new business career providing an absorbing and rewarding future, preserving perhaps for the generations to come, works of art that would have otherwise, in their damaged condition, have been gathered up and consigned to the oblivion of the waste-paper basket.

Suggested entries in restorer's reference notebook

No. of piece   **Date**
No. 42   27 January 1980
Name and address of owner
Mr John Smasher,
12 Bow Hall Road,
Chelsea SW3
Tel No.:
Date work commenced 15 July 1980
Brief description of piece
Derby Teacup decorated with a 'Japan' pattern in red, blue and gold. Circa 1880
Condition: Broken in three pieces, small chip missing from rim. Riveted. Some staining.
Repair required: Breaking down old repair – cleaning and removing stains and rivets. Rebonding – making up and replacing missing piece – filling in cracks and rivet holes.
Notes and remarks
Solvent and materials used for breaking down old repair:
Agent used for removal of stains:
Adhesive used   length of setting time:
Fillings used:
Type of paint used (stoving or air-drying):
Colours used:
Type of glaze used:
Problems, if any, and steps taken to overcome the problems:
                Date completed 20 October 1980

Specimen page for restorer's ledger

No. 43   29 April 1980
Mrs I. Dropper
24 Church Lane,
Maidstone, Kent.   Tel No.
One pastille burner (cottage)
Staffordshire porcelain
Pale cream glaze, some crazing and gilding. Yellow and orange flowers, clumps of moss.
Condition:
Previous repair (3 pieces)
Three chips missing from base; several flowers missing; two clumps of moss missing, chips missing from chimney
Repair:
Cleaning and taking apart old bonding
Rebonding
Making up and replacing (1) several flowers; (2) two clumps of moss; (3) pieces of chimney; (4) two large chips in base; (5) one small chip in base.
Repainting and glazing.
Estimated cost:
Remarks:
Date completed:
Date collected:

GLOSSARY OF TERMS AND TECHNIQUES

Abrasives
Papers or files used for polishing and smoothing. Start with coarse grades moving on to finer grades until a smooth surface has been obtained.

Adhesives
Gums, glues and pastes made up of various animal or chemical substances to form a sticky material which, when applied to surfaces that are brought into contact with each other, will create a firm bond. When used with different filler powders will produce a putty-like composition for filling in missing pieces. Also called cement.

Airbrush
An instrument used to spray paint on to the restored area of porcelain by means of compressed air at the rate of 20-30 psi (2·76-4·14 mks).

Baking
Drying the painted piece of porcelain or pottery under heat in a domestic oven or similar apparatus.

Bloom on varnish
Moisture in the varnish when it is sprayed on to the porcelain will cause it to have a cloudy appearance. This is known as 'bloom'.

Bonding
Joining two broken pieces of ceramic together by means of an adhesive.

Breaking down
Breaking apart an old repair by dissolving old adhesive with appropriate solvent.

Building up
Applying putty-like composition to a piece of ceramic in order to replace missing areas.

Burnishing
Polishing gold leaf with an agate, celluloid or leather tool in order to improve the gloss.

Carborundum
An abrasive stone (silicon carbide) used for smoothing

	down composition, usually in the form of a small wheel used with a drill.
Casting	Producing a facsimile of an original model by making a mould of the model and filling the mould with a liquid substance which will harden into the shape of the mould.
Casting material	See **Composition**.
Catalyst	Substance used with resins and with certain glazes to facilitate a change in their original state.
Cold setting	Paints, enamels, and glaze mediums which dry at room temperatures and do not need baking.
Composition	Mixture of adhesive and powder fillers, or water and powder fillers forming substance of varying consistency for making casts from moulds; for modelling up missing parts; for filling in cracks and missing chips.
Crackle	A fine tracery of hairline cracks found in the glaze of certain types of Chinese porcelain and also some European

	porcelain, e.g. Staffordshire.
Crazing	Cracks found on the surface of some European porcelain.
Decoration	Adornment or embellishment: patterns and designs painted on the ground colour of the porcelain; patterns and designs applied in gold paint or gold leaf; raised mouldings.
Dowel	Headless pin made from a length of stainless steel wire, brass wire or glass cut to size.
Dowelling	The positioning of a length of wire or pins into holes in the ceramic, in order to strengthen the bond of two pieces of ceramic, or as a means of joining a limb to the body of a figurine, or to strengthen a handle when replacing it.
Drilling	Making holes in porcelain or pottery by means of an electric drill and diamond-pointed drill heads.
Feathering	The technique of gradually fading out the painting on a restored area, so that it blends with the undamaged area.

Filing down	Rubbing down the dried composition with abrasive papers and files to a smooth surface.
Fillers (filler powders)	Powders such as kaolin, dental plaster, titanium dioxide etc., which are mixed with epoxy resin to make a putty-like composition for filling in cracks and missing chips.
Gilding	The application of gold, gold leaf in particular.
Glaze	The glass-like protective coating on the surface of the piece which imparts a lustre of varying densities. The glaze is usually made from a mixture of lead, potash, borax and sand, which when fired melts and merges with the piece, forming an outer coating on the surface of the ceramic.
Glaze medium	A clear lacquer, usually supplied with its own solvent and thinner.
Glazing	The application of a hard, shiny, protective, translucent medium over the dry painted area.
Glue	Another term for adhesive, used usually in connection with the older types of adhesives.
Key	The roughness of the surface of a layer of either paint or composition which assists in the adhesion of the subsequent layer. The term is also used when making a two-part mould to describe a small protuberance which is made to fit into a corresponding hole to ensure the two pieces align perfectly.
Locking out	Occurs in assembling and bonding several broken pieces when the final piece will not fit into place owing to the incorrect order in which the pieces have been bonded.
Medium	The substance, e.g. water or oil, with which pigments are blended for painting.
Mending	Repairing a broken piece.
Modelling	The making-up of missing pieces without the use of a mould. This is also called freehand modelling.

'Mother'	The hard outer plaster support on a rubber latex mould to make it extra rigid.	**Pressed moulds**	Moulds made by pressing the moulding material on the area to be reproduced.
Mould	A shape taken from a model in rubber latex or a harder substance, into which a casting material is poured to make a reproduction of the model.	**Putty**	See **Composition**.
		Reinforcing	Strengthening the broken area by means of dowels.
Overglaze	The decoration is applied after the piece has been glazed. In early soft-paste porcelain, pigments were used that did not require fixing at a high temperature.	**Releasing agent**	Substance used to prevent two sections of a mould from adhering to each other.
		Restoring	Bringing a broken piece of ceramic as far as possible back to its original state.
Overspray	The hazy edges that appear on either side of the painted area in spray-painting, if the air pressure is faulty or needle adjustment is required.	**Retouching**	Painting in decorations in repaired areas.
		Rivet	A small metal bolt fitted into holes which have been drilled into the porcelain. The bolts are then clenched to bond the broken pieces securely together.
Pigments	Substance used for colouring. Mineral, animal or vegetable substances which, when mixed with a medium (water or oil), will form a paint.		
		Sanding	Rubbing down dried composition with sandpaper or other abrasive papers of varying grades in order to obtain a smooth surface.
Pinning	The length of wire or dowel which is placed into the appropriate hole to form the stub on to which a missing limb will be modelled up.	**Solvents**	Substances used for reducing or dissolving the consistency of another substance (e.g. paint, adhesive) by means of a

chemical reaction. It is important to ascertain that the substance to be removed or thinned will mix easily with the solvent. Care should be taken when removing varnish with a solvent that the paint beneath will not be lifted off and, if applying a varnish thinned with solvent, that the paint will not lift on application of this varnish and thinner mixture.

Spraying   Painting on to ceramics with an airbrush.

Sprung   When the rim of a broken piece of ceramic is so warped that it cannot be fitted back into its original position it is described as being sprung.

Stippling   Applying paint by dabbing with a fine pointed brush on to the area to be painted.

Stoving   Drying the bonded and painted piece by means of applying heat either in a domestic oven or some similar apparatus. Use special stoving paints.

Strapping   The holding together of the bonded pieces with adhesive tape to keep them firmly in place while the adhesive dries.

Support   A device, either of plaster of Paris or pads of modelling putty which keeps a bonded piece in position until the adhesive has dried.

Swabs   Pieces of cotton wool dipped in the appropriate solution, bleach or solvent, and placed over the area requiring treatment.

Tacky   When the varnish or lacquer becomes sticky and not quite dry it is described as tacky.

Thinner   Solvent used to dilute paints and glaze medium.

Tinting   The addition of pigment colour to glaze, usually in small amounts.

Transfer printing   A form of decoration first used in the early eighteenth century in Europe. The design was engraved on thin copper plate, then transferred on to the ceramic and fired at a low temperature.

Undercut	The space between the embellishment on the ceramic (flowers, figures etc.) and the ceramic itself. When there is much undercut, it is difficult to make an easily removed mould of the ceramic.
Underglaze	The decoration is painted on to the piece before glazing. It is fired, then glazed and fired again, thus making the decoration permanent.
Varnish	Usually a resin in solution with alcohol or turpentine. Moisture in the varnish will create bloom.

LIST OF MATERIALS, TOOLS, EQUIPMENT AND SUPPLIERS

Cleaning Materials		**Suppliers**
Acetone	A colourless liquid produced from a process of distillation of wood and other substances. A powerful volatile solvent. Removes old paint and varnish. Cleans edges before bonding. Dissolves cellulose adhesives. Highly inflammable. Do not inhale.	F. W. Joel Ltd. Green & Stone of Chelsea Chemists (in small quantities) *Hardware stores* *City Chemicals, N.Y.* *Conservation Materials Ltd.*
Ammonia 880 (*Ammonia 28%*)	A cleanser and water softener used for removing grease and dust from porcelain surfaces. It is a compound of hydrogen and nitrogen. Diluted 1 part ammonia to 10 parts water, it is a safe cleanser. A few drops of ammonia added to a solution of hydrogen peroxide 100 Vol. (1 part to 3 parts water) makes a good bleach and removes stubborn stains from porcelain. Causes burns and skin irritation. Handle with care.	F. W. Joel Ltd. Hopkins & Williams Green & Stone of Chelsea *City Chemicals, N.Y.*

Amyl acetate	Banana oil. A clear liquid with a strong distinctive smell of pear drops. A good solvent for cellulose paints, lacquers and varnish. Ethyl acetate is a similar substance.	F. W. Joel Ltd. Hopkins & Williams *Conservation Materials Ltd.*
De-Solv 292 (*Cured Epoxy Dissolver*)	A volatile, non-flammable for dismantling epoxy resin joints.	F. W. Joel Ltd.
Distilled water	Non-ionic water for washing ceramics.	Chemists Garage accessory stores *Supermarkets* City Chemicals, N.Y.
Ferroclene (*Naval jelly*)	Used to remove rust marks left by rivets and metal embellishments. Dilute 1 vol. to 1 to 2 vols water. Causes burns and skin irritation. Handle with care.	F. W. Joel Ltd. Green & Stone of Chelsea *Hardware stores*
Hydrogen peroxide 100 vol. (*Hydrogen peroxide 30–35%*)	A liquid obtainable in a solution of water. When used with 3 parts water and a few drops of ammonia 880 (*ammonia 28%*) it is a good bleaching agent. Poison. Exercise caution when handling. Can cause severe burns.	F. W. Joel Ltd. John Bell and Croyden Green & Stone of Chelsea *City Chemicals, N.Y.*
Methylated spirits (*denatured ethyl alcohol*)	Used for smoothing the surface of fillings in building up and in modelling. Cleans tools.	Most chemists *Conservation Materials Ltd.*

Nitromors (green label) (*Methylene chloride*)	Non–flammable paint remover based on methylene chloride. Removes paint, varnish and dissolves old adhesives including shellac and rubber–based adhesives. Causes burning if in contact with the skin. Wash in cold water.	Ironmongers D-i-y shops *City Chemicals, N.Y.*
Sepiolite (*Magnesium trisilicate*)	Pure hydrated magnesium silicate mixed with water to a thick paste and applied to stained area will remove stains from stone or marble.	F. W. Joel Ltd. *City Chemicals, N.Y.*
Sodium hydroxide	Also known as caustic soda. In a solution with water (1 part soda to 5 parts water) it is used for breaking down old bonds and also for cleaning porcelain and glass.	F. W. Joel Ltd. Chemists *City Chemicals, N.Y.* *Conservation Materials* *Ltd.*
Synperonic NDB (*Triton X100*)	Non-ionic detergent for cleaning ceramics.	F. W. Joel Ltd. *City Chemicals, N.Y.*

Adhesives

Araldite (2-tube)
 (*Devcon Clear*)
	Epoxy resin for bonding. When mixed with filler powders forms good composition for fillings.	Hardware and d-i-y
		   stores
		 Green & Stone of
		   Chelsea
		 Epoxy Technology Inc.
		 Hardware stores

Araldite AY103/HY956 (*Epotek 301 and* *hardener or RP103* *and hardener H956*)	Epoxy resin. Mix 5 parts AY103 to 1 part hardener HY956. Mix 4 parts Epotek 301 or RP103 to 1 part hardener. Strong adhesive for bonding. Good for fillings and castings when mixed with appropriate filler powders.	Ciba-Geigy Ltd. F. W. Joel Ltd. Green & Stone of Chelsea *Epoxy Technology Inc.* *Conservation Materials* *Ltd.*
Cyanoacrylate Resin Adhesive Loctite 15496 (*Eastman 910 or* *Permabond*)	Instant impact adhesive. Not to be used with fillers. Used with good effect when bonding jade or glass. Keep the container well sealed and store in a cool dry place. Shelf life 12 months. Avoid contact with the skin.	F. W. Joel Ltd. Green & Stone of Chelsea *Stationers* *Hardware stores*
Evostick 'W' (*Titebond glue*)	Use as in Vinamul 6815 for bonding pottery and stoneware.	Hardware and d-i-y stores *New York Central* *Supplies*
Sintolit (*Pliacre*)	A transparent white cold quick-setting polyester adhesive. Used for bonding earthenware as it does not get drawn into the porous body. Do not use if stoving.	F. W. Joel Ltd. Green & Stone of Chelsea
Vinamul 6815 (*Jade 403*)	Polyvinyl acetate emulsion (PVA). Used for bonding pottery and stoneware. Can be used with plaster of Paris and powder pigments for colouring when filling and building up.	F. W. Joel Ltd. *Talas*

Fillers

Barytes powder (*Barium sulphate*)	For giving body to composition when mixed with adhesive resin.	Hopkins & Williams F. W. Joel Ltd. Green & Stone of Chelsea *City Chemicals, N.Y.* *Conservation Materials Ltd.*
Beeswax	Melt and mix with plaster of Paris for filling alabaster. Highly inflammable.	F. W. Joel Ltd.
Dental plaster (*Hydrocal*)	For mixing with adhesive to make a composition for filling and building up missing pieces. Also used for casting and as a support for moulds.	Alec Tiranti Ltd. *Rower Dental Supply*
Kaolin powder (*china clay*)	A fine white powder formed from the mineral feldspar. Makes a good composition when mixed into adhesive. Has a dark grey finish, but with the addition of titanium dioxide an ivory-coloured finish is produced.	Hopkins & Williams F. W. Joel Ltd. Chemists *City Chemicals, N.Y.* *Conservation Materials Ltd.*
Ketone Resin N	For combining with microcrystalline wax for use as a filling for alabaster.	F. W. Joel Ltd.

Marble flour (*marble powder*)	Mix with Araldite adhesive for a good strong filling for porcelain. With Vinamul makes a good filling for stoneware. Has a slightly gritty texture.	F. W. Joel Ltd. *A. Ace Von Damm Co*
Microcrystalline Wax Cosmolloid 80H (*Victory White*)	Used with Ketone Resin N as a filling for alabaster.	F. W. Joel Ltd. *Conservation Materials Ltd.*
Plaster of Paris	A fine powder made from gypsum. Mix with adhesive to make a composition for filling and building up missing pieces. Also used for casting and as a support for moulds.	Chemists
Plastogen G (*Clearcast*)	A metholacrylate resin with hardener for filling in cracks and missing chips in glassware.	F. W. Joel Ltd. *City Chemicals, N.Y.*
Polyester casting resin	A filler for glassware.	Alec Tiranti Ltd.
Polyfilla (interior) (*Polyfix*)	A cellulose filler which is mixed with water to a thick paste. An ideal composition for filling and building up pottery.	Hardware and d-i-y stores *Conservation Materials Ltd.* *Hardware stores*
Polyfilla (fine surface) (*Polyfix*)	Used as a final application to Polyfilla fillings for a smooth finish after rubbing down.	Hardware or d-i-y shops *Conservation Materials Ltd.*

Sylmasta (*Elmer's Epoxy Resin*)	A two-part putty. When mixed together makes a good composition for filling in and replacing missing pieces in ceramics.	Hardware and d-i-y shops The Sylglas Co.
Titanium dioxide powder	An opaque and brilliantly white pigment powder. Mixed with Araldite adhesive it produces a strong white filling and composition for building missing pieces. Also prevents adhesive from yellowing.	F. W. Joel Ltd. Green & Stone of Chelsea John Bell & Croyden *City Chemicals, N.Y.*

Moulding materials

Mercaptan Impression Material	Used for pressed moulds. Sets in approximately 7 minutes.	F. W. Joel Ltd. Green & Stone of Chelsea *Rower Dental Supply*
Paper dust	Filling for rubber latex to strengthen mould. Mix to the consistency of a creamy paste.	F. W. Joel Ltd.
Plasticine (*Plastelina Roma Italian No. 2 white*)	Plastic-like modelling putty useful for pressed moulds and for supporting pieces while bonds are setting.	Art stores *Sculpture House*

Rubber latex
Qualitex PV or
Revultex
(*Kwikmold or Pliatex*)
	A good flexible moulding. Can be stiffened with the addition of paper dust or wood flour and, if necessary supported with a plaster of Paris 'mother'. Not to be used on ivory, metal, marble or painted surfaces.	F. W. Joel Ltd.
		Bellman Ivey & Carter
		Green & Stone of
		  Chelsea
		Adhesive Products Corp
		  (for Kwikmold)
		Sculpture House (for
		  Pliatex)

Slipwax release agent (*Butcher's wax*)	Wax used in two-part moulds to prevent the two parts sticking to each other. Also prevents dental plaster supports sticking to rubber mould.	F. W. Joel Ltd. *Supermarkets*
Vinamold Red (MP 130C–140C)	For two-part moulds and relief moulds with very little undercut. Unpleasant vapour – keep covered and work in a well-ventilated room.	F. W. Joel Ltd. Alec Tiranti Ltd.
Wood flour	Fine sifted sawdust used to mix into rubber latex in order to stiffen it.	Builders' merchants

Polishes

Simoniz Car Polish	A polish for reducing the glaze on ceramics.	Garage shops and hardware stores

Solvol Autosol	Slightly abrasive polish for cleaning ceramics and for reducing the gloss on a glaze.	Garage shops and hardware stores *Conservation Materials Ltd.*

Paints

Artists' oils	Squeeze on to absorbent paper then mix with glaze medium. Can be air-dried or stoved. Obtainable in small tubes.	Winsor & Newton Green & Stone of Chelsea Good art shops *Art shops* *Winsor & Newton* *Pearl Paint Co.* *Rex Art Supplies* *H. G. Daniels*
Chintex paints	For stoving at 104°C (220°F) for 30-40 minutes. Suitable for domestic ware subjected to heat and constant wear and tear. Comes with its own glaze and thinner.	Chintex
Cryla Paints (*Artists Acrylic Colours*)	For use on pottery and objects with a matt surface. Not for pieces in general use or those subjected to heat.	Winsor & Newton Good art shops Green & Stone of Chelsea *Pearl Paint Co.* *Charette Corp.* *Rex Art Supplies*

Humbrol Enamels (*Testors Plastic Enamel Paints*)	Cold setting paints with a fairly wide range of colours.	Humbrol Ltd Green & Stone of Chelsea *Hardware and craft shops*
Mearlin Powder Lustre Pearl Pigments Flamenco Colours	For painting on lustre ware.	Cornelius Chemicals Ltd *Mearl Corp.* *Sparkl-It Co.* *Metalflake Inc.*
Powdered pigments (dry)	Air-drying pigments. Mix with a glaze medium for painting.	Winsor & Newton G. Robertson & Co. Ltd. Green & Stone of Chelsea *Artists' shops* *Winsor & Newton* *Permanent Pigments Inc.*

Glaze mediums

Barbola Varnish	Clear white glaze. Mixes with oil paints and Humbrol Enamels. Not to be used in the air-brush. Solvent is turpentine.	Good Artists' shops Green & Stone of Chelsea
Chinaglaze (Clear Gloss and Satin)	2-pack urea formaldehyde/melamine formal-dehyde lacquer for applying glaze to ceramics.	F. W. Joel Ltd.

	Use with catalyst for air-drying or stove at 50°–60°C without catalyst (though this is not recommended because of its highly inflammable nature).	Phenoglaze Industrial Finishes Ltd. Green & Stone of Chelsea
Chinaglaze (White)	2-pack acid cured lacquer with a matt finish. Use with catalyst for air-drying – tough-dry in 40 minutes. Solvent is Phenthin 83. Highly inflammable so stoving is not recommended.	F. W. Joel Ltd. Phenoglaze Industrial Finishes Ltd. Green & Stone of Chelsea
Chintex Clear Glaze	Use with Chintex stoving paints, also with artists' oils and powdered pigments. Stove at 94°C (200°F) for 1 hour. Solvent – Chintex Clear Glaze Thinner.	Chintex
Humbrol Clear Varnish and Matt Varnish (*Testors Plastic Enamel Varnish*)	Tends to discolour. Solvent is white spirit or Humbrol thinner.	Humbrol Ltd. Model shops Green & Stone of Chelsea
Rowneys Picture Varnish 800	A good glaze surface. Easy to apply. Is not very liable to bloom or yellow with age. Solvent white spirit or turpentine.	George Rowney & Co. Ltd. Good artists' shops Green & Stone of Chelsea

Rustins Clear Gloss Varnish	A good glaze medium does not yellow quickly.	Rustins Ltd.

Thinners and solvents

Chintex Clear Glaze Thinner	For thinning and cleaning.	Chintex
Chintex Thinner	For thinning Chintex paints.	Chintex
Humbrol Thinner	For thinning and cleaning Humbrol Enamels.	Humbrol Ltd. Green & Stone of Chelsea
Phenthin 83	For thinning and cleaning Chinaglaze.	Phenoglaze Industrial Finishes Ltd F. W. Joel Ltd. Green & Stone of Chelsea
Turpentine	For thinning and cleaning oil colours. Thickens on exposure so should be kept away from light.	Winsor & Newton Good artists' shops Green & Stone of Chelsea *Artists' shops*

White spirit (*mineral spirit, Stodard solvent*)	Thins and cleans Humbrol Enamels and oil paints. Good cleaner for equipment.	Artists' shops and hardware stores *Conservation Materials Ltd.*

Gilding materials

Bronze powders	Mix with a glaze medium	George Whiley Ltd. Good artists' shops *New York Central Supply Co.* *Pearl Paint Co.*
Gold powders	Mix with a glaze medium.	George Whiley Ltd. Winsor & Newton Good artists' shops *Pearl Paint Co.* *Triangle Co.* *H. G. Daniels* *Conservation Materials Ltd.*
Tablet gold	Effective in gilding work.	George Whiley Ltd. Winsor & Newton George Rowney & Co. Ltd. *New York Central Supply Co.*

Transfer gold leaf	In book form. Use with glaze medium.	George Whiley Ltd. C. Robertson & Co. Ltd. *New York Central Supply Co.*
Treasure Gold Liquid Leaf	Supplied in bottles. Easy to apply in a selection of shades.	Green & Stone of Chelsea Winsor & Newton *Pearl Paint Co.* *Triangle Co.* *Rex Art Supplies*

Tools and equipment

Abrasive papers	For smoothing down fillings, composition and modelling. Trimite Wet and Dry 320–1000–1200 Flex-I-Grit 320/400/600 Sandpaper (coarse to fine) Flour paper	Hardware stores John Myland Ltd. F. W. Joel Ltd. Green & Stone of Chelsea *Moyco Industries Inc.* *Conservation Materials Ltd.*
Acid-resistant brush	For use with corrosive liquids, e.g. Ferroclene.	F. W. Joel Ltd. *Conservation Materials Ltd.*

Agate burnisher	For burnishing and polishing gold decorations.	George Whiley Ltd.
		 Art stores
		 Winsor & Newton
		 Green & Stone of
		    Chelsea
		 New York Central
		    Supply Co.
		 Conservation Materials
		    Ltd.

Airbrush	For spray painting over large areas of repair. Helps effectively to conceal repairs in porcelain.	Morris & Ingram
		    (London) Ltd.
		 Conopois Instruments
		    Ltd.
		 De Vilbiss Co. Ltd.
		 Colour Sprays Ltd.
		 New York Central
		    Supply Co.
		 Arthur Brown
		 Thayer & Chandler Inc.
		 Badger Airbrush Co.
		 Paasche Airbrush Co.
		 Conservation Materials
		    Ltd.

Apron	To protect clothing.	Department stores
Blades	See scalpel blades.	

Bottles	Various sizes for storing materials. Some should have drip dispenser tops.	Chemists
Bowls	Various sizes, plastic.	Hardware stores
Brushes	Soft bristle nylon washing-up brush, old tooth-brushes, soft brushes, wire brushes for cleaning.	H. S. Walsh Ltd. *Uptown Material House* *Conservation Materials Ltd.*
Callipers	For accurate measurements in modelling and in the duplication of patterns.	Stationers H. S. Walsh Ltd. *New York Central Supply Co.* *Sculpture House* *Sculpture Services Inc.* *Conservation Materials Ltd.*
Carbide abrasive heads and burrs	Use with the electric drill to smooth down composition.	Claudius Ash Sons & Co. Alec Tiranti Ltd. *Uptown Material House* *Starlite Industries Inc.* *Foredom Electrical Company*

Carborundum stone
(*Arkansas stone*)
	For filing and for sharpening tools	F. W. Joel Ltd.
		Alec Tiranti Ltd.
		*Allcraft Tool and Supply
		   Co. Inc.*
		Abbey Materials Corp.
		Uptown Material House
		*Conservation Materials
		   Ltd.*

Cartons, plastic	For mixing and storing.	
Chinagraph pencil (*Volatile crayon*)	For marking ceramics.	Wengers Ltd. *New York Central Supply Co.*

Compressor	Used with the airbrush to build up air-pressure for spraying the paint.	Conopois Instruments
		   Ltd.
		Morris & Ingram
		   (London) Ltd.
		*New York Central
		   Supply Co.*
		Sam Flax
		*Allcraft Tool & Supply
		   Co. Inc.*
		*Conservation Materials
		   Ltd.*

Cooker, table-top, electric	For stoving paints	Department stores

Cotton wool	For rolling on to cocktail sticks for the application of rubber latex; for swabs.	Chemists *Pharmacies*
Creams, barrier	To protect skin from harmful effects of resins, detergents, etc.	Chemists *Pharmacies*
De-ionizing unit such as Elgasat B114 (*Demineralizer such as Illco-way Universal Model*)	For supplying de-ionized water	F. W. Joel Ltd. Elga Products *Fisher Scientific*
Dental tools	For modelling, probing and cleaning out old composition from small holes and crevices.	Claudius Ash Sons & Co. *Rower Dental Supply* *Arista Surgical Supply Co. Inc.*
Diamond-tipped carbide drill heads – Hi-Di 63, 1, 1B	Used with electrical drill for drilling into ceramics	The Glass Studio Claudius Ash *Rower Dental Supply* *Starlite Industries Inc.* *Allcraft Tool & Supply Co. Inc.* *Brookstone Company*

Dividers	For accurate measurements in modelling and drawing designs on ceramics.	Stationers H. S. Walsh Ltd. *Uptown Material House* *New York Central* *Supplies*
Dowels	See Glass and Wire	
Drill with flexible shaft	For making holes in ceramics for dowelling. Also for grinding down composition.	F. W. Joel Ltd. Buck & Ryan Ltd. *Allcraft Tool & Supply* *Co.* *Elm Electric & Hardware* *Co.* *Foredom Electrical* *Company*
Files, needle and riffler	Sets of six to twelve medium to large sizes. For filing down composition and shaping composition in modelling.	Alec Tiranti Ltd. E. Gray & Sons Ltd. Buck & Ryan Ltd. *Allcraft Tool & Supply* *Co. Inc.* *Abbey Materials Corp.* *Uptown Material House* *Conservation Materials* *Ltd.*

Flexible mask, Duralair (*Pulmosan*)	Can be worn over spectacles with no-mist lens. Prevents inhalation of dust and fumes.	F. W. Joel Ltd. Alec Tiranti Ltd. *Olympic Glove Company* *Allcraft Tool & Supply Co. Inc.* *Pulmosan Safety Equipment*
Flex-I-Grit	See Abrasive papers	
Foil, aluminium	For covering pieces when soaking in a solution with evaporates rapidly.	Supermarkets *Hardware stores*
French chalk	For dusting rubber latex moulds to prevent sticking when removing cast.	Good chemists
Glass dowels	For dowelling glassware	Glaziers
Gloves, vinyl	To protect hands against harmful detergents and solvents	F. W. Joel Ltd. *Olympic Glove Company* *Conservation Materials Ltd.*
Goggles	See Flexible mask	
Gravers, diamond, 1.75 cm and 3.50 cm	For modelling and shaping	Ironmongers H. S. Walsh Ltd. *Allcraft Tool & Supply Co. Inc.*

Hacksaw, small size with spare blades	For cutting through difficult rivets.	Ironmongers Buck & Ryan Ltd. *Abbey Materials Corp.* Uptown Material House
Kerrocleanse 22	For removing epoxy resins and paints from the skin.	Alec Tiranti Ltd.
Lamp with flexible arm		F. W. Joel Ltd. H. S. Walsh Ltd. *Artists' stores* *Electrical and hardware suppliers*
Magnifying glass	For examining repaired areas for defects	Opticians *Conservation Materials Ltd.* *New York Central Supplies*
Measuring glasses and measuring spoons	For measuring adhesives and solvents.	Chemists *Pharmacies*
Modelling tools, boxwood	For modelling and shaping.	Artists' shops Alec Tiranti Ltd. *Sculpture House* *Sculpture Services Inc.*

Palette knife	For mixing adhesives and paints.	Artists' shops Alec Tiranti Ltd. *Artists' stores* *New York Central* *Supplies*
Paint brushes, sable	Sizes 00 to 3. Flat for glazing.	Winsor & Newton Art shops *New York Central* *Supply Co.* *Sam Flax* *Conservation Materials* *Ltd.*
Pens, waterproof	For marking porcelain	F. W. Joel Ltd.
Pliers, flat-nosed and pointed	For cutting dowelling wires and removing stubborn rivets.	F. W. Joel Ltd. H. S. Walsh Ltd. *Allcraft Tool & Supply* *Co. Inc.* *Uptown Material House* *Conservation Materials* *Ltd.*
Respirator, Duralair, fitted with dust/mist filter (*Pulmosan E453 and E454*)	For protection against fumes and dust particles.	F. W. Joel Ltd. *Olympic Glove Company* *Allcraft Tool & Supply* *Co. Inc.*

		Eastern Safety Equipment Co. Inc. *Pulmosan Safety Equipment*
Riffler files	See Files	
Ruler	For measuring	Stationers
Saucepan with lid	For heating Vinamold	Hardware stores
Scalpel handles, nos. 3 and 4 Scalpel blades nos. 10, 11, 15, 23	For cutting dried composition, for filling and many other uses.	Alec Tiranti Ltd. F. W. Joel Ltd. *Uptown Material House* *Talas* *New York Central Supplies*
Scissors, stainless steel, one sharp pointed, one blunt pointed, 10 cm	For cutting and various other uses.	Department stores Needlework shops
Sellotape (*Scotchtape*)	Adhesive tape for strapping bonded pieces together.	Stationers
Sellotape dispenser	To facilitate the cutting of the tape into various lengths.	Stationers

Spatula, metal, Scopas Nos. 47 and 48	For mixing adhesives, filling and modelling.	Alec Tiranti Ltd. *Sculpture House* *Sculpture Services Inc.*
Tiles, ceramic, plain white and dark colours	For mixing and matching colours for hand and spray painting. Also for mixing adhesives.	D-I-Y shops Builders' merchants *Guirdanella Bros.*
Tweezers	For picking up small objects, e.g. small chips. Also for taking up cotton wool swabs from bleach and harmful solvents.	H. S. Walsh Ltd. *Uptown Material House* *Abbey Materials Corp.* *Conservation Materials Ltd.*
Vice, medium size and pin vice	To fit on to workbench to hold work when both hands need to be free. Also for holding dowels and wire for cutting.	Ironmongers Alec Tiranti Ltd. *Uptown Material House* *Abbey Materials Corp.* *Conservation Materials Ltd.*
Wire for dowels, brass (gauges 16, 18, 19) and stainless steel	For pinning missing limbs and strengthening bonds.	H. S. Walsh Ltd. J. Smith & Sons (Clerkenwell) Ltd. P. Ormiston & Sons Ltd. Renown Special Steels Ltd. *Magnet Wire Inc.* *T. E. Conklin Co. Inc.*

Wire cutters	For cutting wire dowels.	H. S. Walsh Ltd. J. Smith & Sons (Clerkenwell) Ltd. P. Ormiston & Sons Ltd.
Wooden cocktail sticks	For stirring and applying adhesive. For probing and modelling and many other uses.	Supermarkets

—NAMES AND ADDRESSES OF— SUPPLIERS IN THE U.K.

(An asterisk indicates that the supplier produces a catalogue)

Armstrong Cork Co.,
Kingsbury,
London, NW9

*Claudius Ash Sons & Co.,
58 Whytecliffe Road,
Purley,
Surrey, CR2 2AW

Bellman Ivey & Carter & Co.,
358A Grand Drive,
Wimbledon,
London SW20 9NQ

Buck & Ryan Ltd.,
101 Tottenham Court Road,
London, W1P 0DY

*Chintex,
Wraxall,
Bristol, BS19 1JZ

Ciba-Geigy Plastics Division
Ltd.,
Duxford,
Cambridge, CB2 4QA

Colour Sprays Ltd.,
62 Southwark Bridge Road,
London, EC1

Conopois Instruments Ltd.,
The Airbrush and Spray
Centre,
39 Littlehampton Road,
Worthing, BN13 1QJ

Cornelius Chemicals Ltd.,
Ibex House,
Minories,
London, EC3

*DeVilbiss Company Ltd.,
47 Holborn Viaduct,
London, EC1A 2PB

Elga Products,
Lane End,
Bucks.

The Glass Studio
West Pallant
Chichester PO19 1TD

E. Gray & Sons Ltd.,
Grayson House,
12-16 Clerkenwell Road,
London, EC1M 5PL

Green & Stone of Chelsea,
259 Kings Road,
London, SW3
(Green & Stone of Chelsea
specialize in materials for china
restoration)

Hopkins & Williams,
Freshwater Road,
Chadwell Heath,
Essex.

Humbrol Ltd.,
Marfleet,
Hull, HU9 5NE

F. W. Joel Ltd.,
PO Box No. 6,
Downham Market,
Norfolk, PE38 9ED

(F. W. Joel exports to many
countries including Australia,
South Africa, Canada and the
U.S.A.)

John Bell & Croyden,
50 Wigmore Street,
London, W1H 0AU

★Morris & Ingram
(London) Ltd.,
156 Stanley Green Road,
Poole,
Dorset, BH15 3BE

John Myland Ltd.,
80 Norwood High Street,
London, SE27 9NW

P. Ormiston & Sons Ltd.,
Broughton Road,
London, W13 3BH

Phenoglaze Industrial
Finishes Ltd.,
466 London Road,
Croydon, CR9 2TY

Renown Special Steels Ltd.,
Eley Estate,
Nobel Road, Edmonton

C. Robertson & Co. Ltd.,
Parkway,
London, NW1 7PP

George Rowney & Co. Ltd.,
12 Percy Street,
London, W1A 2BP
and
PO Box No. 10,
Bracknell,
Berkshire

Rustins Ltd.,
Drayton Works,
Waterloo Road,
London, NW2

J. Smith & Sons
(Clerkenwell) Ltd.,
42-54 St John's Square,
Clerkenwell,
London, EC1P 1ER

The Sylglas Co.,
61 Knights Hill,
London SE27 0HL

*Alec Tiranti Ltd.,
70 High Street,
Theale,
Berks.
and
21 Goodge Place,
London W1P 2AJ

Union Carbide UK Ltd.,
Chemical Division,
PO Box No. 2LR
8 Grafton Street,
London, W1A 2LR

H.S. Walsh Ltd.,
12-16 Clerkenwell Road,
London, EC1M 5PL

Wengers Ltd.,
Etruria Works,
Garner Street,
Stoke-on-Trent,
Staffordshire, ST4 7BQ

George Whiley Ltd.,
Victoria Road,
South Ruislip,
Middlesex HA4 0LG

Winsor & Newton,
51-52 Rathbone Place,
London W1P 1AB
and
Wealdstone,
Harrow, HA3 5RH

NAMES AND ADDRESSES OF SUPPLIERS IN THE U.S.A.

*Abbey Materials Corp.,
116 West 29th Street,
New York,
N.Y. 10001

A. Ace Von Damm Co.,
900 Grand Street,
Brooklyn,
N.Y. 11211

Adhesive Products Corp.,
1660 Boone Avenue,
Bronx,
N.Y. 10460

Allcraft Tool & Supply Co.
Inc.,
22 West 48th Street,
New York,
N.Y. 10036

Arista Surgical Supply Co. Inc.,
67 Lexington Avenue,
New York,
N.Y. 10010

Badger Airbrush Co.,
9125 West Belmont Avenue,
Franklin Park,
Illinois 60131

Brookstone Company,
'Hard to Find Tools',
121 Vose Farm Road,
Peterborough,
N.H. 03458

*Arthur Brown,
2 West 46th Street,
New York,
N.Y. 10036

Charette Corporation,
31 Olympia Avenue,
Woburn,
Ma. 01888

City Chemicals,
132 West 22nd Street,
New York,
N.Y. 10011

T. E. Conklin Co. Inc.,
324 West 23rd Street,
New York,
N.Y. 10011

*Conservation Materials Ltd,
Box 2884,
340 Freeport Boulevard,
Sparks,
Nevada 89431

H. G. Daniels,
2543 West 6th Street,
Los Angeles,
California 90057

Eastern Safety Equipment Co.
Inc.,
45-17 Pearson Street,
Long Island City,
N.Y. 11101

Elm Electric and Hardware
Company,
871 Sixth Avenue (31st Street),
New York,
N.Y. 10001

Epoxy Technology Inc.,
56 Grove Street,
Watertown,
Mass. 02172

Fisher Scientific,
52 Fadem Road,
Springfield,
N.J. 07081

Sam Flax,
35 East 28th Street,
New York,
N.Y. 10016
and
250 Sutter Street,
San Francisco,
Cal. 94105

*Foredom Electrical Company,
Bethel,
Conn. 06801

Guirdanella Bros.,
4 Bond Street,
New York,
N.Y. 10002

Magnet Wire Inc.,
25 Walker Street,
New York,
N.Y. 10013

Mearl Corp.,
41 East 42 Street,
New York,
N.Y. 10017

Metalflake Inc.,
P.O. Box 950,
Haverhill,
Mass. 01830

Moyco Industries Inc.,
21st and Clearfield Avenue,
Philadelphia,
Pa. 19132

*New York Central Supply Co.,
62 Third Avenue,
New York,
N.Y. 10003

Olympic Glove Company,
465 South Dean Street,
Englewood,
N.J. 07631

Paasche Airbrush Co.,
1909 West Diversey Parkway,
Chicago,
Illinois 60614

Pearl Paint Co.,
308 Canal Street,
New York,
N.Y. 10013

Permanent Pigments Inc.,
2700 Highland Avenue,
Cincinnatti,
Ohio 45212

Pulmosan Safety Equipment,
30-48 Linden Place,
Flushing,
N.Y. 11354

Rower Dental Supply,
331-337 West 44th Street,
New York,
N.Y. 10036

Sculpture House,
38 East 30th Street,
New York,
N.Y. 10016

*Sculpture Services Inc.,
9 East 19th Street,
New York,
N.Y. 10003

Sparkl-It Co.,
12131 Magnolia Boulevard,
No. Hollywood,
Ca. 91607

*Starlite Industries Inc.,
1111 Lancaster Avenue,
Rosemont,
Pa. 19010

Talas,
Division of Technical Library
Service,
104 5th Avenue,
New York,
N.Y. 10011

Texas Art Supply,
2001-21 Montrose Boulevard,
Houston,
Tx. 77006

Thayer & Chandler Inc.,
442 North Wells Street,
Chicago,
Illinois 60610

Uptown Material House,
50 West 47th Street,
New York,
N.Y. 10017

Winsor & Newton Inc.,
555 Winsor Drive,
Secaucus,
N.J. 07094